Penguin Handbooks
Chinese Food

Kenneth Lo is a graduate of Yenching University, Peking,
and Cambridge University, England. In his time he has
been a student of English literature, diplomat, fine art
publisher, journalist, lecturer, professional tennis player,
and now Chinese food critic and cookery writer.

His close association with the spread of Chinese food in the
West dates back to the last war, when as a welfare and
industrial relations officer attached to the Chinese Consulate
in Liverpool he organized a number of restaurants for the
many disabled Chinese seamen. As a pioneer in this field
he later assisted many of his friends to get their catering
enterprises on their feet in London during the 1950s.

In the 1960s he was for several years an Inspector of
Chinese restaurants for the Egon Ronay Guide, and he is
currently the Chinese consultant to the Good Food Guide
of Britain. As a 'professional eater' of nearly a decade's
standing, he has eaten more widely in Chinese restaurants
than any man, 'in his right mind would have cared to!'

His other books on Chinese cookery are: *Peking Cooking*,
Quick and Easy Chinese Cooking, *Cooking the Chinese
Way*, *Best of Chinese Cooking*, *Complete Chinese Cookbook*
(awaiting publication). He is currently writing *Chinese
Vegetable and Vegetarian Cooking*, *Cheap Chow* and
Chinese Cooking for Health.

He is a founder director of the Chinese Gourmet Club of
London, which assists members to choose the best selection
of Chinese dishes and guides them to the best eating-places.

KENNETH LO

Chinese Food

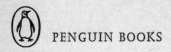 PENGUIN BOOKS

Penguin Books Ltd, Harmondsworth,
Middlesex, England
Penguin Books Inc, 7110 Ambassador Road,
Baltimore, Maryland 21207, U.S.A.
Penguin Books Australia Ltd, Ringwood,
Victoria, Australia

First published 1972
Reprinted 1973
Copyright © Kenneth Lo, 1972

Made and printed in Great Britain by
Cox & Wyman Ltd,
London, Reading and Fakenham
Set in Linotype Juliana

Contents

PART ONE

Chinese Food

There is a basic difference between eating in the Chinese style and eating in the West. In western meals the dishes are eaten consecutively; a soup following on hors d'oeuvre, then a main dish, followed by a dessert, or a selection of cheeses, winding up with coffee. This is a pattern which does not vary very much for a party meal at home or a mayoral banquet.

A Chinese family meal is essentially a spread, with all the dishes, whether fish, fowl, meat, egg, vegetables or soup, brought to the table at the same time. Since all the dishes are highly savoury, rice is eaten throughout the meal to cushion and absorb this savouriness, as well as to provide bulk.

A feeling of well-being and satisfaction is an essential part of a good Chinese meal. Curiously enough, eating for eating's sake was a preoccupation of many Chinese in the past, despite the country's poverty. Probably because of the limitations or absence of other entertainment, eating as a form of recreation became a major pastime.

The Chinese have always been uninhibited about their food, perhaps because they are aware of its important place in their cultural heritage. Chinese ladies will modestly turn their faces to the wall when their amateur operatic performances hit the high-notes, but I have yet to see a Chinese lady, who does not present her culinary creations beaming with pride and her face wreathed in smiles – completely confident of her guests' appreciation.

At parties and banquets in China the food is served in the

western manner, one dish after another. On these occasions people eat for pleasure more than for sustenance, and so rice or steamed buns (the staple food of the North) are not served – except perhaps towards the end, to help settle the stomach. At such feasts there may be anything from a basic 10 or 12 to 20 or more dishes. Traditionally there should be 300 dishes served at a great 'Manchu-All-China Banquet', so the choice and sequence of dishes for a Chinese banquet often require greater thought and arrangement than a corresponding western meal.

In this book I shall describe the two main types of Chinese meal: the banquet and the ordinary main meal, as well as the Chinese breakfast and tea or tea-house snacks, which are eaten either for tea or for light lunches.

For daily meals there is no great difference between the dishes served at lunch time and at dinner. Assuming that the family is not existing at subsistence level, but is able to eat reasonably well, a Chinese lunch or dinner would consist of 4 or 5 dishes with one or two soups.

Cooking Methods

Soups

If there are two soups at the meal, one will be meaty and the other probably a plainer vegetable soup. Most Chinese soups have a meat broth base, even vegetable soups, which often consist of chopped vegetables suspended in meat consommé, sometimes with the addition of a few dried shrimps, dried scallops, or dried vegetables (such as dried mushrooms and tree-fungi) which have been simmered in the broth. The other popular soup is egg soup, often called egg-drop or egg-flower soup, in which drops of beaten egg have coagulated into flowerets in the simmering meat broth. Chopped chives or spring onions, a pinch of M.S.G.,* pepper, a drop or two of vinegar and any other appropriate seasonings are added.

Chinese soups are always tasty and refreshing, never heavy; clear rather than thick. They are not meant to be filling. Their function is to complement and help down rice, which is bland and neutral and to provide a refreshing change of texture after savoury food, rather than act as a meal in themselves. In a way, soup replaces water on the Chinese dinner table. Tea is sometimes served throughout a Chinese meal to supplement soup, or it can take the place of soup as an even blander liquid refreshment between mouthfuls of savoury foods. To appreciate the nuances of flavour of the different combinations of ingredients, it helps if one can start each mouthful afresh, the more so when eating for entertainment rather than purely from necessity. In winter the Chinese like to warm themselves up fast by spooning down mouthfuls of hot soup alternately with other foods. Pretty soon the whole body glows comfortably, even in the arctic temperatures of a north China winter. We Chinese find it strange that in the West, where soups are drunk independently of other dishes, few people have tried the combination of savoury soups with savoury foods. In a sense, it is a Chinese variation of the western custom of drinking different wines throughout a meal, and it is worth trying, if only for the new gastronomic experience.

Meat Dishes

The Chinese prepare their meat dishes in the main in seven different ways:

*Monosodium glutamate, sometimes called *veh t'sin,* flavour powder or gourmet powder.

quick stir-fried (usually diced, in slices, or shredded)
red-cooked (stews)
clear-simmered (long cooking)
deep-fried or dry-fried (usually in batters)
crystal boiling
hot-plunging
hot-assembled

Quick Stir-frying

In the quick stir-fry method of cooking one or more types of meat is cooked in combination with vegetables, or other thinly sliced or shredded foods. Because of all the permutations, this method accounts for by far the largest number of dishes. It is also one of the most economical forms of cooking. Firstly, in terms of heat, total cooking time is seldom more than 10 minutes and often less than 5 minutes. Secondly, for stringent economy, a good proportion of vegetables can always be substituted in a dish, and the amount of meat reduced to a minimum. So it is not surprising that most restaurant cooking falls into this category both in China and abroad. Apart from being highly economical, quick stir-frying gives the chef an opportunity to display his virtuosity by giving him plenty of scope, e.g. in combinations, seasoning, and multi-phase cooking (the acceleration and deceleration of heat in a short time). Every individual dish is a challenge which any good artist or chef welcomes.

In quick stir-fried cooking, a small amount of chopped onion with even less ginger or garlic, or both, are usually first fried together in a little oil. When the oil has absorbed the taste and aroma of onion and garlic, etc., the main ingredients are added (pre-sliced, pre-seasoned, or pre-marinated) and vigorously stirred with a metal spoon, spatula, or a pair of bamboo chopsticks as they fry for a minute or two over the high heat.

The cooked meat is then removed while the shredded or sliced vegetables, and, frequently, a small amount of soaked, dried vegetables for added flavour, are fried in the same oil for a minute or two. At this point more oil can be added if necessary and slight adjustments of seasoning be made; e.g. a dash of salt just as the vegetables are sweating from contact with the hot pan will accentuate their greenness.

After the vegetables have been stir-fried for a minute or two the meat is returned to the pan and stir-fried together with the vegetables. At this point a little broth and wine can be added which, apart from preventing burning, since all the cooking is done at very high heat, will also help to provide a small amount of gravy or sauce. This sauce is frequently thickened with a few teaspoonfuls of cornflour (2–3 teaspoons) mixed in a small quantity of water and given a lift with a minute amount of M.S.G. or a couple of drops of sesame oil for aroma.

The resultant sauce is nameless, but is an important and integral part of the dish and can be varied and modified in hundreds of ways, depending upon the combinations of different ingredients, their relative quantities, and the types and quantities of seasonings and basic sauces used.* One characteristic of the quick stir-fry sauce is that it is rich in the natural juices of the main ingredients and reflects their flavour distinctively.

Red-cooking

Red-cooking is also very popular in China. Its popularity is due to the unique qualities of soya sauce, and its happy adaptability to almost any form of food, whether meat, fish or fowl. Soya sauce is probably the one single item which above all distinguishes Chinese cooking from western cooking. A

* Soya sauce, shrimp sauce, hoisin sauce, oyster sauce, etc.

mixture of soya sauce, with a sprinkling of sugar, some dry sherry, salt, M.S.G., chopped ginger, garlic and onion is a basic addition to many dishes, and makes almost any kind of meat tasty and appetizing. The same applies to vegetables. I suspect that a great many western stews would be immeasurably improved by the addition of this basic soya herbal sauce. A jelly can be made by simmering meat or poultry with the skin and bones in the mixture. This then becomes a sort of master sauce in jelly form which has an even stronger flavour than the basic mixture and is especially good for quick-frying vegetables.

In red-cooking the meat or poultry is first quick-fried and then simmered in broth or water along with soya sauce and other constituents of the soya herbal sauce (including one or two pieces of star-anise and a sprinkling of cinnamon to give the dish added character). Tender cuts of meat or young poultry only take 30–40 minutes, but tougher meat or old birds need longer to be cooked to perfection. Since long, slow cooking in soya sauce does not change the character of a dish, red-cooking is ideal for such cuts as shin of beef, pork knuckle, or pork trotters, and makes a rich and succulent dish. Cuts of this kind will require as much as $1\frac{1}{2}$–$2\frac{1}{2}$ hours slow simmering. The Chinese are extremely fond of the savoury meat jelly, rendered down by long, slow cooking of the skin and fat: pork, with the skin attached, is often cooked in this manner.

As I have already mentioned, the character and quality of most Chinese dishes have to be considered in relation to rice or steamed buns. The red-cooked dishes, which are usually served with lots of gravy, are especially popular – rice soaked in gravy is quite as tasty, and more filling than the meat itself.

The red-cooked dishes have the added advantage for the housewife that they can be cooked well in advance, for they are just as good a couple of days later. In the summer they can be refrigerated and eaten cold, with the larger chunks of meat sliced, and served with the jellied gravy. The sensation of jelly melting against the hot rice in your mouth must be unique to Chinese eating, like the warm, many-scented earthiness which rises in waves from the land when the snow first starts melting in the spring. The nascent flavour of the jelly seems to be enhanced by being freshly released.

Not all red-cooked dishes are necessarily served swimming in gravy. In some cases the gravy can be reduced (as in French cooking), and the neatly sliced meat is then dry-fried.

In the case of fish, which does not usually require prolonged cooking, the pieces of fish (or the whole fish) are lightly floured and quickly fried, and then cooked for 5–10 minutes in soya herbal sauce, along with some spring onion, a tablespoon of dried prawns, a few strips of sliced ham (with fat), and a few pieces of soaked, dried mushrooms. The exterior of the red-cooked fish is a rich brown in colour, and, when the flesh is broken into with a pair of chopsticks, it flakes off in pieces of pure white – a contrast which seems to enhance the freshness of the fish and the tastiness of the sauce and exterior. The gravy from a red-cooked fish dish has a taste and quality all of its own, often more delicious than meat gravy. In the far western province of Szechuan and in the southern coastal areas this fish gravy is used extensively for cooking and flavouring.

Clear-simmering and Steaming

The aim of clear-simmering and steaming is the same: to make the food very tender and very pure.

The Chinese usually use earthenware casseroles for clear-simmering. There is even a famous restaurant in Peking called the 'House of Earthenware Casseroles' (Sa Kuo Chü) where all the food is cooked in earthenware casseroles. This method of cooking originated with the Chinese Moslems of north China who inhabited the great grasslands and prairies of Inner Mongolia and Sinkiang which stretch towards the very heart of Central Asia. Here the cattle were often cooked whole, and the recipes from these parts tend to reflect the simplicity nomadic life enforced. Nowadays, when the meat is very tender, it is sliced into smaller pieces to be eaten with a variety of dips and mixes to give piquancy. Sometimes the meat is given a short, sharp fry after being sliced, which crisps it up. Many people prefer this type of plain cooking, where you can mix your own dips, to those dishes in which the final flavours and sauces are predetermined by the chef in the kitchen.

For clear-simmering in a modern kitchen a heavy pan or casserole can be used, either in the oven or on the top of the cooker with an asbestos sheet. Clear-simmering is essentially a long drawn-out affair – taking anything from 2–5 hours. The appeal to the Chinese of clear-simmered dishes lies in the unadulterated taste and tenderness of the meat, and also in the incomparable consommé which comes with the dish, and is usually served in a large tureen.

Fresh vegetables – often in quite large quantities – as well as a considerable amount of wine can be added during the last half hour of cooking; the former absorb all the flavours of the consommé and at the same time give a freshness to the whole dish, while the wine gives the whole ensemble delicious over-tones which are very heaven to the rice-eater!

Duck and chicken are cooked in this manner, as well as lamb, beef, goat, pork, and sometimes whole fish. The poultry is often cooked with 1 lb. or more of Chinese cabbage* placed under the bird during the last 30–40 minutes of cooking.

---

* Cabbage with the quality of celery, now easily obtainable in America and in parts of Britain; if not available, substitute celery.

The dish is made more interesting by adding small quantities of such ingredients as dried mushrooms, dried scallops, mussels and one or two slices of fresh ginger (the latter is added to lamb, beef, poultry and fish, but not pork). Turnips and carrots are often used instead of Chinese cabbage, especially with mutton and beef. These root vegetables can of course stand much longer cooking than cabbage, and can be put in the pot or casserole an hour before the dish is done. Turnips are widely used as a vegetable in China, and are not primarily for feeding livestock. In clear-simmered dishes and in soup making they are a recognized and regular accompaniment to beef.

Steaming is a common method of preparing the so-called 'turned-out' meat dishes. These are prepared in much the same way as western steamed puddings: steamed in a heat-proof bowl and then turned out for serving. For turned-out dishes, the meat is cut into strips roughly 2 ins. × 1 in. × ¾ in., usually with skin attached at one end, and packed into a heatproof bowl skin-side down. Various appropriate seasonings and layers of salted and dried vegetables are then added, and in some cases salt fish is placed on top. The finesse lies in the care with which dried and salted foods are combined with sauces and seasonings to give the maximum interest and contrast to the final dish. The bowl of meat is steamed for 1–2½ hours, and, by the time it is cooked, the various flavours from the dried and pickled foods and seasonings and sauces have seeped through the whole mass of meat, which by then is jelly-like and tender. A small amount of wine can be added for extra flavour. When this meat pudding is turned out on to the serving dish the skin side of the meat is on top, forming a layer of skin-jelly which is especially succulent and attractive (at least to the Chinese!).

In the western province of Szechuan the peasantry have developed this style of cooking to a fine art. In the famous

Three Steamed and Nine Turned-Out Dishes three lots of the same type of meat are packed with three different combinations of flavourings and other ingredients in three different bowls, and all steamed together in the same steamer. When the dishes are all cooked, you have a tour de force – one sort of meat in three different dishes, each with its distinctive flavour.

Westerners are often intrigued by the Chinese basket steamers arranged like piles of top hats in layers, one on top of the other, so that the steam rising from the rice boiler at the bottom (since rice has to be cooked in any case), forces its way through all the layers of baskets to the very top, and all the dishes are cooked simultaneously. These basket steamers can be 2 ft wide, so quite a number of prepared dishes can be parked on each 'floor' (like cars in a multi-storey car park) and all cooked together. You can imagine that with five layers of baskets and three dishes on each 'floor', you can cook a veritable banquet in one go!

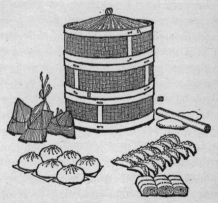

One must, of course, put the dishes which require least cooking in the top basket and those which require most in the lowest one, just above the boiler.

Steaming is also used in China to give the final seal to a dish prepared from ingredients which have already been cooked separately. In other words, various pre-cooked items are assembled in the same container and given, as a final process, a short blast of steam (say, for 10–15 minutes) to achieve the necessary unity. For example, one type of Eight Jewel Duck, composed of numerous ingredients, which are variously flavoured by simmering in master-broth and by deep-frying, is finally subjected to prolonged steaming to make the duck meat very tender.

Making a mess is one of the pitfalls of quick stir-frying, but since steamed dishes are left undisturbed during cooking and do not suffer the final great stir-up, they can be attractively arranged and presented more easily.

Deep-frying and Dry-frying

Deep-frying and dry-frying are less common in China than the methods already described. This is probably because oil is so expensive compared to air or water! One seldom sees a special deep-fryer in China; the Chinese use the same pan for deep-frying as for other kinds of cooking. It is called wok in Cantonese. This is a round frying-pan with sides sloping towards a central well. It is a bit like a coolie-hat turned upside down. A wok is particularly suitable for quick stir-frying, as it is much easier to toss, turn and stir vigorously without spilling in such a pan, than in an ordinary frying-pan. The wok is also economical for deep-frying, since, with its small base and sloping sides, a small amount of oil goes a long way. A few tablespoons of oil are usually enough, and the food is simply turned over in the central well of oil, using a flat wire spoon, and left on the sloping sides of the pan to drain as well as to continue to cook. In some dishes the food is cooked first on one side, then on the other (like fried bread) in a small amount of oil, using a flat pan as in the West. This method is called *Chien* or *Tieh* as opposed to *Ts'a*, or deep-frying.

For deep-frying the meat or poultry is often chopped and dipped in batter. The batter helps to seal in the juices during cooking. Seasoning and marinating the meat in advance improves the flavour, and, of course, the better the quality of the meat, the better the result. One of the best-known dishes cooked this way is Eight-Piece Deep-fried Chopped Chicken. Actually, the young chicken is usually chopped, not into eight, but into a dozen or more pieces, and then dipped in batter before frying. Large prawns are often cooked in a similar manner, leaving the tail free of batter, both for easier handling and because it will turn a decorative red. Game, poultry, and meat are sometimes salted or marinated and hung for a day or two, and then rinsed and dried before being battered and fried. These additional steps help to tenderize and flavour the meat. Minced meat balls, fish balls and prawn balls are often deep-fried or semi-deep-fried. As a point of interest, the principal difference between Chinese meat balls and western meat balls is that the Chinese invariably mix chopped water chestnuts and a small proportion of chopped fat with the minced meat to give the meat balls a crunchier texture and more succulent flavour.

At table, one of the most popular dips for battered deep-fried foods is the salt and pepper mix, which is simply a mixture of coarse salt and freshly ground pepper heated for a moment or two on a dry pan, a technique which gives the mix a distinct bouquet.

Dry-fried dishes are cooked without batter. Meat is usually well seasoned and marinated, or may have been braised first in a gravy reduced until all the liquid evaporated. At this point a small quantity of oil, and a few other ingredients are added to the pan for a final quick fry, perhaps with a little wine or soya sauce. During this last stage of cooking an extremely tasty crust of sauce and meat juice will form. Sometimes the final cooking is by slow heating on a dry pan. Because of their piquancy, dry-fried foods do not need any table dips, although sometimes plum sauce, tomato sauce or sweet and sour sauce are used to supplement or provide contrast to the spicy crust.

Crystal-boiling

The practice of heating food in a pan of boiling water, and then removing the pan from the heat after a minute or two so that the cooking is completed by the retained heat is, I think, original to China. I am calling this method crystal-boiling after Crystal Chicken, which is cooked in this way. For very young and tender chickens the Chinese allow no more than 1 minute of boiling before the pan is removed from the fire. The bird is cooked by the heat retained in the water, in which it stands for a few hours to cool, before it is drained and chopped into pieces of appropriate size. Crystal Chicken is often served with dips based on soya sauce with such additions as vinegar, chopped ginger, garlic, sherry or chilli.

If longer cooking is required for Westerners, the food is brought to the boil for 1 minute, allowed to cool for 20 minutes, and the process is repeated a couple of times. In the case of pork, to convert the fat to a palatable jelly the periods of boiling or simmering have to be much more prolonged, and the whole process really resembles clear-simmering.

In any case, meat or poultry which has been crystal-boiled is seldom over-cooked, or tough. Moreover, if the meat or bird was well chosen (young, tender, and very fresh, so that a degree of under-cooking does not detract from the dish), the result is richer in natural juices than if it were cooked in any other fashion. The final combination at table of these juices with the various dips and mixes is a gourmet's delight. Among the half dozen or so dishes on a well-appointed Chinese table there is often a dish prepared in this manner.

Hot-plunging

A variation of crystal-boiling is hot-plunging. Hot-plunging involves plunging thin slices of fish or meat in water or broth which is kept at a rolling boil. This can be done either in the kitchen or at the dining table, using a Peking hot-pot, a type of charcoal burner, or a fondue cooker which burns spirit. Mongolian lamb hot-pot is a famous dish where the guests each cook their own bite-sized portions of food at the table, one mouthful after another (something like fondue bourguignone), and end up by drinking the tasty soup from the hot-pot (which by now has absorbed the flavour of all the pieces of meat which have been cooked in it). Drinking the soup is then the crowning glory of the meal.

Hot-plunging is easily done in the kitchen in a casserole. The meat or fish is very thinly sliced, seasoned and marinated and sprinkled lightly with cornflour. The broth is usually a vegetable soup made by cooking some vegetables (both dried and fresh) in a meat broth base. This soup is then brought to a rolling boil and the sliced meat or fish is scattered through the liquid for not more than a minute of rapid boiling. The dish can be served in the earthenware or metal pan in which it was cooked or transferred to a large, flat, pre-heated bowl. As a rule the proportion of liquid to meat or fish should not exceed 3:1 (or less), since the dish is not primarily meant to be a soup. This method of cooking is called *tang pao* which, literally translated, means soup-exploded! Alternately, for even lighter cooking, the boiling soup is simply poured over the seasoned foods in the serving bowl and served.

Hot-assembled Gravy Dishes

There is one type of Chinese dish which has no counterpart in European cooking. These dishes are composed of various ingredients cooked together and served in a bowl with plenty of thickened soup or gravy. Although westerners do mix gravy with their mashed potatoes and eat the mixture with relish, the Chinese equivalent of mixing various sorts of gravy with rice and other absorbent foods, is much more sophisticated, if not more refined! Special dishes, which I have called hot-assembled gravy dishes, have even been created for the purpose. The Chinese term for this type of preparation is *h'ui* which means bringing together or meeting. The Chinese character includes a sign indicating fire or heat which is reflected in my term hot-assembly.

In a successful dish of this kind there must be harmony and balance between the ingredients – otherwise it degenerates into a mess, which, as I have said before, one must always avoid in Chinese cooking.

The basis of a *h'ui* dish is a selection of fresh vegetables (including some pre-fried bean curds cut into ½in. squares, or transparent pea-starch noodles, which absorb a lot of gravy) together with a small selection of dried foods (such as dried mushrooms, lily buds, fungi, shrimps, scallops, etc.) and some pickles and a drop or two of aromatic sesame oil. A good quantity of gravy previously prepared and cooked separately adds extra flavour to the vegetables, and the transparent noodles, or small bean curd cakes, harmonize the whole conglomeration of flavours. Such dishes are always cooked with plenty of gravy (say ½–¾ pint to 2–3 pints of food), slightly thickened with cornflour or water-chestnut flour, and seasoned with a couple of tablespoons of wine or sherry, a drop or two of sesame oil and, optionally, ½–1 teaspoon M.S.G. The large, steaming hot, aromatic tureen, swimming in gravy, is always a very welcome sight at a Chinese dinner table. It is always tackled with great gusto irrespective of the other dishes which have been provided. These gravy dishes are something which we Chinese miss most when we are abroad and obliged to rely on western food for any length of time.

There is a famous Chinese dish prepared in this manner called *lo-han chai*, which is a hot-assembly of various vegetables and vegetarian foods and very popular in dining halls of temples and monasteries (where it originated) throughout China.

The *lo-hans* are the minor gods of the Chinese temples and monasteries, who sit all around the temple-hall in their thousands at the feet of the Buddha. A suitable translation would be Dish of the Minor Gods. If western vegetarians, using health foods and fresh vegetables made a dish borrowing the methods of *lo-han-chai*, they would be very pleasantly surprised.

For non-vegetarians, the dish is a tour de force: the taste of meat diffuses through a conglomeration of vegetables, which have been flavoured with dried and pickled foods. It is a bit like a grander version of chopsuey which has, of course, never been heard of in China, and is regarded – even by Chinese abroad – as very inferior.

Fish Dishes

Fish usually needs much less cooking than meat, whether in China or the West. In China, fresh ginger and onion are always used to help get rid of the fishy flavour, or else the fish may be fried (or deep-fried) before it is given a more fancy treatment. As I have already mentioned, we seldom really deep-fry anything. Fish fried in onion and ginger-impregnated oil (sometimes with garlic as well) will lose its fishiness, even if only a small amount of oil is used. Fish which is not fishy is meat as far as the Chinese are concerned, and tender meat at that; and by and large it is enjoyed much more when it has been so treated and flavoured.

Fish as Meat

Because we like to regard fish as meat, we cook it in much the same way as meat, only for a shorter time. We red-cook it, quick-fry it, clear-simmer it, deep-fry it, steam it, and hot-plunge it, but we do not crystal-boil or hot-assemble it. The well known and popular sweet and sour sauce is often poured on fish after it has been deep-fried until the outside is crisp. Sometimes this sauce is made hotter and more piquant by adding chilli peppers or chilli oil.

Quick-frying and Wet-frying

Quick-fried fish is not usually stir-fried vigorously like meat or vegetables, for the obvious reason that it would break up if it were treated so violently. Quick-fried fish is usually sliced into thin slices about $2\frac{1}{2}$ ins. × $\frac{1}{6}$ in. × 1 in., lightly dusted with flour or dipped in a light batter of cornflour and egg white, and then fried on both sides like English fried bread. The sauces are only added afterwards. Chicken broth with some white wine and dash of sugar and thickened with cornflour is a favourite, or the classic sweet and sour sauce hotted up with a little chilli. A little wine sediment paste may be added to one of the above sauces to give a winey tang. Sometimes the sliced fish is simmered for a while in the familiar soya herbal sauce, which may even have been made with meat gravy. In all these sauces, sliced or chopped fresh ginger is added either during the frying or at the sauce-making stage. It is absolutely essential when quick-frying that the fish is extremely fresh, otherwise it will flake, and disintegrate. As long as you can obtain very fresh fish, and once you have got used to cutting fish into comparatively thin slices, you can prepare and cook first class dishes in a matter of minutes.

The whole fish (or large pieces of it) can also be fried and served with sauce. Whole fish or large pieces are treated by the Chinese much as westerners treat a joint: the fish is brought steaming to the table on a large oval dish or silver salver, rich and gleaming with sauce, for the host to dismember with a pair of chopsticks and share among the guests. Yellow River Carp is a famous dish which is brought to the table audibly crackling from the contact of sweet and sour sauce poured over the sizzling hot, deep-fried fish.

Steaming

One of the very best Chinese fish dishes is the straightforward steamed whole fish (be it mullet, carp, bream, bass, perch or salmon). The fish is rubbed inside and out with salt and fresh ginger, and then decorated and marinated for anything from 10 minutes to an hour before steaming. About 2 teaspoons of sugar can be used in the marinade, together with some wine, vinegar and soya sauce. Strips of shredded ham, pork or bacon (both lean and fat – the latter being important too), dried mushrooms (soaked and shredded), dried shrimps, lily buds, and spring onions are used for garnishing. The eventual flavour is as important as the presentation. (Sliced lemon and pimento are also recommended.) When the fish has been decorated and marinated, it is placed in a steamer for 15–25 minutes depending upon the size of the fish.

The flesh of a fish marinated and steamed like this is sweet and fresh and firm. An Indian cartoonist friend, who has travelled in most parts of the world, once told me he thought the gravy from such a fish was one of the tastiest things he had ever eaten – and this at the height of the Indo-Chinese border crisis when very few things Chinese appeared commendable to an Indian!

Smoking

Another popular method of cooking, or rather flavouring fish in China, is smoking. In contrast to the western practice, smoked fish is usually cooked in one way or another beforehand – most frequently by red-cooking or dry-frying. Smoking is then, in effect, a finishing process. The pieces of fish are placed in a large container and permeated with the smoke produced by sugar, sawdust, or tea-leaves smouldering over hot charcoal. In the West the most convenient method is to burn tea leaves, sugar or sawdust on a sheet of tin foil placed in a large, old saucepan, with the fish placed on a rack immediately above. The pan is heated over high heat until the sugar, tea leaves, etc., start to smoke heavily. The fish is then left in the closed saucepan for varying periods (average 10–15 minutes) for the smoke to flavour and adhere.

Smoked fish (or meat) is often served cold in China as an hors d'oeuvre.

Drunken Foods

Another popular way of serving cold fish or meat is to have them 'drunken'. The food is heavily seasoned and marinated for a few hours or overnight, and then, after rinsing in fresh water, quickly steamed or lightly simmered. Then it is drained and dried, and steeped in wine (or sherry) for a period ranging from a day to a week (though 2–3 days is the average), and cut into appropriate sized pieces ready to serve. Drunken poultry, meat, or fish ought to be a hit in the West; it just needs to be popularized.

I wonder if there are corresponding western dishes where food which already has quite a characteristic taste is then both highly seasoned and steeped in alcohol? The Chinese are expert at multi-phase flavouring and cooking foods, and the practice of first smoking and then marinating in wine makes for highly complex and interesting taste sensations.

N.B. Expert cutting and carving of meat, fish and vegetables, and elegance in arrangement are given more attention in the presentation of the Cold Dish than any other dish. Larger pieces of smoked or drunken foods are neatly cut up into bite-sized pieces and arranged elegantly on the serving dish. Apart from the easily acceptable taste of the majority of items in the Cold Dish, this care in presentation is, I think, why Chinese hors d'oeuvres could most easily and successfully be transported to the West when the whole repertoire of Chinese cuisine becomes better known and more widely accepted.

Vegetables and Vegetarian Cooking

Chinese vegetarian cookery is a world of its own with its extensive monastic background and time-honoured Buddhist traditions. On the other hand, non-vegetarian treatment of vegetables, like the Chinese way with fish, is closely related to the cooking of meat. This perhaps, above all, makes Chinese vegetable dishes so appetizing, though quick-frying, which retains so much of the original authentic taste and crunchy texture of the vegetables, also contributes. The combination of meat flavours and fresh vegetables creates a special appeal for the palate, and the connoisseur of Chinese food delights in vegetable dishes as much as in fish or meat dishes.

The common denominator in Chinese vegetable cookery and fish cookery is the use of chicken broth or 'high broth'. This broth is made by simmering chicken and pork spare ribs together (see p. 90). For plainer or simpler home cooking, the basic soya herbal mixture, pepped up with a slice or two of fresh ginger, is the most popular addition. In fact, one of the favourite and tastiest Peking dishes is red-cooked cabbage which is cooked in precisely this mixture. Its counterpart, white-cooked cabbage, consists of cabbage simmered in strong chicken broth or high broth, suitably seasoned with salt and pepper, pepped up with a few slices of ginger and dried shrimps and half a teaspoon or so of M.S.G. Small quantities of white wine are added if desired, and the broth is thickened with cornflour, and whitened with milk (a small addition of butter and cream is recommended in the West). In more elaborate versions the milk is mixed with finely minced breast of chicken. Chinese cabbage is often prepared in one of these ways. (Where Chinese cabbage is not available, use celery or the crinkly-leaved Savoy cabbage.) A large amount of rice can be eaten with it, without resorting to meat, which should not be missed even by inveterate meat eaters, as many of us are.

Dried and Pickled Vegetables as Flavourers

Apart from flavouring vegetables with meat or meat juices (gravies), the Chinese have explored and developed a wide area of cookery where pickled, dried, and salted vegetables and fungi (rather than herbs) are used extensively for flavouring. Dried pre-soaked mushrooms, for example, are used widely. Anyone who has used dried mushrooms will have noticed that they have much more flavour than fresh mushrooms, which seem pretty insipid in comparison. In Chinese cooking over 90% of the mushrooms are dried, and mushroom-water is one of the principal bases of the broth used in Chinese vegetarian cooking. The fresh mushrooms, which are so prized in western cuisine, are very much relegated to second place in Chinese food.

Quick Stir-fried Vegetables

For vegetables cooked by the quick stir-fry method, onion,

garlic, ginger, or pickles are often first fried in the oil so that it absorbs their flavours. The vegetables and seasonings are added when the oil has become well impregnated; salt added at this stage helps turn the vegetables greener. It is only when the vegetables are glistening with oil that any sauce or broth (and then only in small quantities) is added to enrich or vary the dish. Since the whole process of quick stir-frying seldom exceeds 3–5 minutes depending on the type and quantity of vegetables used, much of the goodness and the original flavour of the vegetables is retained.

Hot-assembly

Another popular method of cooking vegetables is by hot-assembly. The vegetables are first stir-fried separately with different flavourings, and then hot-assembled in the pan. Wine, M.S.G., and sesame oil can all be added during the final assembly to improve the flavour and the aroma of the dish. This method of cooking produces a veritable bouquet of vegetables as aromatic as a great bunch of sweet-smelling flowers.

Steamed Vegetables

Even the tougher vegetables can be cooked in this manner if the dish is placed in a steamer after the assembled frying. Since the vegetables will by then already be well-oiled and glistening, a short, sharp period of steaming will not spoil their appearance, and it will allow them to absorb the seasonings and sauce fully while the hot steam will make them much more tender. In this case steaming completes the cooking process.

Hot-assembly and steaming are methods used primarily for mixed vegetable dishes where the flavours of many fresh and dried vegetables are blended together, usually after they have been individually quick-fried. Steaming and hot-assembly are employed as the last *unifying* process.

Pure Vegetable Dishes

Pure vegetable dishes contain only one or two vegetables and they are often steamed with a reasonable amount of broth. The vegetables are parboiled or quick-fried first, seasoned, and then arranged in an attractive pattern in a large deep dish, garnished with a few slices of ham, dark strips of dried mushrooms (soaked and sliced), and a spoonful or two of dried scallops (or their dried root muscles). The whole dish is then placed in a steamer for 15–20 minutes to tenderize the ingredients and unify them without spoiling their appearance. As with most steamed dishes, the appearance and presentation of the foods can be pre-arranged before steaming starts. When it is cooked the dish is brought to the table intact.

This cooking method can be used not only for pure vegetable dishes, but also for mixed vegetable and meat dishes (a majority of Chinese dishes).

A certain steamed dish from Nanking called Vegetable Basket, consists of a ring of hearts of spring greens, standing like sentinels round the sides of a flat-bottomed tureen, and surrounding a cluster of vegetables which is built up like a small bouquet in the centre of the dish. The dish is meant to portray the freshness and lushness of spring, but, as with all Chinese dishes, at least as much thought is given to its flavour as to its appearance; for, in the Chinese tradition, appearance is second to taste.

One of the favourite Chinese white sauces for vegetables is the *fu-yung* sauce, which is made from minced chicken mixed with broth, egg white, cornflour, and some milk or cream. The vegetables are seasoned, lightly fried or steamed until almost tender, and then finally turned and stir-fried in the white sauce, which makes them attractive and very appetizing. (This technique could well be incorporated into western cuisine.) The greenness of the vegetables contrasting with the whiteness of the sauce is as pure as jade against the rich brown dishes which are so common on the Chinese table.

Poultry

Duck

Although one of China's better known dishes, Peking Duck, is roasted, roasting in the western style is not common in China. For one thing, an oven is a rarity in a restaurant kitchen, let alone in a family home. For another, an oven which is fired not with gas, but with charcoal, can be as complicated as a pottery kiln, and requires more skill to handle than cooking the food itself! The original Peking recipe for cooking Peking Duck included a full-scale description of building and firing the oven, and, with the other aspects of preparation, ran to nearly 15,000 words! Stripped of the finesse and refinement, I found that Peking Duck did not originate in Peking, but came from Inner Mongolia. As a dish it only attained fame in Peking in the last century. Even the oldest restaurant in Peking with Peking Duck on the menu, the Pien Yi Fang, only started to cook and serve it in 1855.

Apart from the selection of the finest duck, which is reared and fattened specially for the purpose, the secret of the dish is in its crackling skin and the way it is eaten. The skin is crisped by the very simple process of dousing the duck with boiling water and thoroughly wiping it down with absorbent cloth or paper, and it is then hung to dry for a few hours or overnight in an airy place, before it is roasted. While it is roasting the bird is not basted at all (in a western oven the door should not be opened at all for 1 hour while the bird roasts at a moderate to hot temperature.)

When the duck is ready, its crackling skin is sliced off and brought to the table together with pieces of sliced duck meat. The crackling skin and meat are wrapped in pancake rolls (in the shape of sleeping bags with the bottom end closed), together with one or two stalks of spring onion, a few strips of cucumber, and a liberal spread of plum sauce. It is the combination of the crackling skin with the tender meat, the crunchy and strong-tasting with the aromatic, the rich with the sweet and sour, which makes this dish a gastronomic experience.

Apart from Peking Duck there are, of course, a good many other well-known duck dishes in China. Some of them claim to be even better than Peking Duck, but the majority of them do not have a crackling skin and do not require such precise timing or skill in fire-building.

The Aromatic and Crackling Duck of North China is prepared by a process of marinating, steaming, and deep-frying. In a majority of restaurants the process is simplified by simmering first in soya herbal sauce and deep-frying the duck just before the dish is served.

Cantonese Roast Duck is roasted filled with liquid or sauce, and it is this duck which is most often seen hung in the windows of Chinatown restaurants abroad. It has a rich, glazed, brown skin, from which it is sometimes known as lacquered duck. The glazed effect is achieved by basting with a mixture of malt sugar (or honey), soya sauce and water or vinegar at intervals of 20 minutes during roasting. Because the duck is filled with liquid it requires at least 30 minutes longer roasting than Peking Duck. Such roasting is usually carried out in a restaurant, in a tall oven, in which 6–8 birds are roasted at a time. The bird is hung upside down with the neck tied up tightly so that no liquid escapes. The tail-end too is securely sewn up, so that nothing leaks out. The duck is usually filled with stock with varying quantities of chopped spring onion, garlic, ginger, tangerine peel and added salt, sugar, honey, sherry, cinnamon and pickles. (I see no reason not to add orange and pineapple too.) Since this liquid will boil and explode if overheated, the roasting can start at a high temperature (400°F, gas 6), but the heat has to be tapered off to about 350°F, gas 4, for the last hour. The duck is usually chopped up and the liquid served as a gravy.

Another famous Chinese duck dish is Hangchow Soya Duck which is salted and steamed. The duck is first rubbed inside and out with ginger and salt, and then placed in an earthen pot and pressed for 72 hours with a 30 lb. weight, changing the position every 24 hours. After the three days' marinade in salt, the duck is rinsed in fresh water, thoroughly dried, and then submerged in soya sauce for another 72 hours, again under a weight with three changes of position. The duck is then cooked in boiling soya sauce for two short minutes.

After draining, a bamboo or wooden cross is placed inside the cavity of the duck to keep it extended and well aired. It should then be hung in the sun for 2–3 days to dry. The cooking method used for Hangchow Soya Duck is open steaming. An average 4 lb. duck should be steamed for 2 hours, when the duck will be ready to be carved or chopped into small pieces and finally re-assembled – more or less anatomically – and served.

The best home-cooked duck I know of is Home-cooked

Greens and Onion Simmered Duck, which consists simply of stuffing the cavity of the duck with 6–7 oz. of segments of spring onion, 2 oz. of dried mushrooms (soaked), a few slices of fresh ginger, a few slices of smoked ham, deep-frying it for 2–3 minutes and then simmering it in a good broth for 1 hour. After the simmering the duck is steamed. The sides of a large tureen are lined with 4–6 hearts of spring greens, each cut in half, the duck is placed in the middle and the skimmed broth from the pan is poured over them all. The tureen and bird are then placed in a steamer and steamed vigorously for 30–40 minutes. The seasoning can be adjusted as you go along. The dish is very wholesome; strong flavours of the onion and the dried mushrooms amalgamate with the richness of the duck, and both contrast with the freshness of the greens. The resulting soup is both rich and fresh. Such a dish is served in a large bowl or tureen and lives up to the highest culinary expectations of a Chinese family gathering.

Chicken

Chicken is much more universally used in China than duck and its meat is much more versatile. A chicken dish of one sort or another is served virtually every day in any well-to-do Chinese family. Chicken can be cooked in most of the ways as meat and duck. Recipes for chicken run into the hundreds. Chicken is in many ways akin to pork, the most widely eaten meat in China. Its particular neutrality means it can be cooked and combined successfully with almost any other meat, fish or vegetable. Because of their similarity, chicken and pork are often interchangeable in different combinations and dishes. Thus there is Chicken Chow Mein and Shredded Pork Chow Mein; Chicken Mushroom, Sliced Pork with Mushroom, Red-cooked Chicken with Walnuts, Red-cooked Pork with Walnuts etc.

Some of the best chicken dishes are ones where chicken is cooked on its own, without complications or additions; for example, the old Peking favourite Diced Chicken Quick-fried in Soya Jam, which is a very pure and simple dish of chicken breast diced into ⅓ in. cubes. These are first dredged with cornflour and fried for ½ minute in a small amount of oil and put aside. A small quantity of very finely chopped onion and an even minuter amount of very finely chopped ginger and crushed garlic are then fried in the same oil (plus one additional tablespoonful) for 1 minute over high heat. The heat is then reduced and 2–3 tablespoons of soya jam and a teaspoon of sugar are added. The mixture is stirred slowly until all bubbling has ceased (which means that all moisture has evaporated), and the soya paste and oil have become a thick glistening sauce. The diced chicken cubes are returned to the pan, the heat is turned up, and the chicken cubes are stir-fried quickly until they are coated in sauce. At this point one can sprinkle the chicken with one or two teaspoons of vinegar and sherry. Then it is stir-fried for another half a minute and served.

The chicken cubes which have been cooked for no more than 1½ minutes in all are so tender that they melt in one's mouth. Chicken can be cooked in a similar manner with chilli sauce (it is then called Kung-pao Chicken), tomato sauce, oyster sauce, or any other sauce. The same applies to diced pork cubes, although they naturally require longer cooking. But none seems to attain the same degree of excellence and popularity as the classical combination just described. Compared with this simple chicken dish, all the dishes in which chicken is combined with one vegetable or another, seem fussy and pedestrian (and, unfortunately, these seem to be the dishes normally served in Chinese restaurants abroad).

To return to pure chicken dishes, another very good one is White-cut Chicken, which has been 'wind-cured'. A freshly killed chicken is thoroughly cleaned and rubbed inside and out with a dessertspoon of salt and a teaspoon of freshly milled pepper, and hung up to dry overnight. On the following day a mixture is made with 1½ tablespoons of lard and a similar quantity of salt and pepper mixed together and previously heated on a dry pan for 1½ minutes. This mixture is then rubbed all over the chicken both inside and out. The chicken is then hung up in a dry spot for 10 days after which it is considered sufficiently cured to be cooked.

Just before cooking the chicken is plunged into a pan of boiling water for a 5 seconds wash-down. It can then either be simmered or steamed vigorously for 30 minutes. When ready it should be chopped through the bones into *mah-jong* sized pieces, re-assembled anatomically on a dish and served.

This Wind-cured White-cut Chicken is quite a speciality in China; it has a taste and quality all of its own and not to be confused with ordinary White-cut Chicken, which is simply crystal-boiled or just lightly boiled, chopped anatomically, sprinkled with a little sesame oil and served with a soya sauce-ginger dip. The same sprinkle and dip can be used for Wind-cured White-cut Chicken, but additional dips such as sherry-soya dip and chilli-soya dip are also recommended.

Before leaving the subject of chicken, there is one type of chopped fried chicken from Fukien which I particularly miss since I have been abroad. It is another pure chicken dish, consisting of chopped chicken fried in wine sediment paste. This paste is made from wine sediment mixed with a small amount of fermented ground rice, and is usually bright red in colour. The pieces of chicken are rubbed in a small amount of salt and lightly fried in a few tablespoons of oil for 3–4 minutes, then removed and drained. A tablespoon of finely chopped onion and a teaspoon of chopped ginger and crushed garlic are then fried for 1 minute in the same pan with a further tablespoon of oil. Then 2–3 tablespoons of the 'paste' are added and stirred into the oil. When the oil, paste, and onion have amalgamated, the pieces of chopped chicken are returned to the pan and are turned and stirred in the mixture over high heat until every piece is covered with the bright red sauce. The resulting aromatic and colourful dish is very tempting. Duck, which requires an extra 2 minutes' initial frying, can be cooked in the same 'paste' with equal success. So can large prawns and small slices or cubes of fish previously fried in batter. Seafoods, such as scampi or scallops, can be fried together with cubed chicken, creating a delicious dish called Fried Dragon and Phoenix: the seafood represents the Dragon and the chicken the Phoenix.

Wine sediment paste is still extremely difficult to obtain in the West. An ersatz version, which works very well, can be prepared by mixing 1½ tablespoons finely chopped onion with 1 teaspoon ground rice, 1 teaspoon sugar, 2 teaspoons hoisin sauce, 1½ teaspoons well-chopped ginger, 1 clove crushed garlic, 2 tablespoons vegetable oil, 2 tablespoons tomato purée, 1 tablespoon finely chopped red pimento and 6 tablespoons dry sherry. Heat and stir the mixture together over low heat until the volume is reduced by ½–⅔. Stir in 1½ tablespoons brandy and leave the mixture to stand until required. This gives sufficient 'paste' to use with 2–3 lb. of chopped chicken or duck.

Food cooked in this paste can be eaten cold, and is an excellent variation both in colour and flavour from smoked fish, jellied meat, sliced soya-simmered meats, marinated vegetables, and other foods served as part of the Chinese Cold Dish.

Chinese Meals

Having made a rapid and sweeping survey of the range of Chinese food, and glanced briefly at the main techniques used in preparing chicken, duck, fish, meat and vegetables, let us see how the Chinese arrange and serve their meals.

Party Dinner

As I said at the beginning, party dinners or banquets occur with great frequency in China among those who can afford to eat well. When the guests are ushered into the dining room, four to six cold dishes will already be on the table waiting.

The hors d'oeuvres usually consist of smoked dishes, 'drunken' dishes, jellied meat, sliced soya-cooked meat, abalone and seafood and exquisitely sliced and marinated vegetables, which were formerly all delicately and attractively arranged on small dishes. Nowadays, however, all the food is more frequently arranged in a flower-like pattern on a large single dish. Indeed, the most attractive thing about Cold Dishes is the harmonious complementary or contrasting colours of the finely cut foods as much as their delicate, subtle flavours. Several shades of green set off the rich brown of the meats and the bright red of dishes cooked in wine sediment paste; the pink contrasts with the pale white-cut meats or chicken and the ivory of the abalone and the marinated celery. The appetites of the diners are immediately whetted by this beautiful display of delicious foods, this artistic array of savouries, which must merit a high place in the world's culinary achievements.

Before the dinner actually begins, the ultra-courteous host goes around with a pewter pot of warmed wine and drinks the health of each of his guests. If the gathering is less formal, he simply waves his chopsticks like a marshal's baton to the guests on his left and right to indicate 'Let's get started'. Although all the proceedings are conducted with restraint and courtesy, occasionally hunger and greed get the better of ritual politeness. The hors d'oeuvres are generally eaten in small nibbles with accompanying sips of wine. Conversation and pleasantries flow back and forth, and gradually formality melts into conviviality.

However, those who are genuinely interested in food (including all those with large and healthy appetites) will be wondering at the back of their minds what surprises are in store for the evening. For the dishes of a Chinese dinner are normally unheralded and unannounced (there is no menu). The host proudly introduces each new culinary creation for the guests to exclaim over in delight. Although the range and number of Chinese dishes is well-nigh unlimited, most of the dishes served at a dinner party are likely to fall within a certain range and pattern. What the diners will look forward to is the chef's interpretation of well-known dishes or 'pieces', with an occasional unusual or surprise dish. The surprise may be derived from a little-known recipe, or something which has just come on to the market after many months out of season, or a dish or food which is normally only found in quite a different region of China, such as ham from Yunnan, or melon from Urumchi, or fresh lichees in Peking in the winter. When the chef is cooking anything from a dozen to a score of dishes for a single meal, he can easily get carried away, and on the spur of the moment create something which comes as a surprise even to the host. If the dish comes off well everybody is pleased, and the chef is congratulated, otherwise some slightly deprecating, if witty, remarks will be made.

It is only when the hors d'oeuvres are over that we move on to the cooked dishes. The first four are usually called *chiu ts'ai* or wine-accompanying dishes, for wine is drunk along with these dishes and between courses. These dishes are usually quick-fried rather than soup dishes, and may be quite dry and crisp, and particularly suitable with wine; for example, Prawn Balls, Sesame Seed Sprinkled Prawns on Toast, Dry-fried Eight-Piece Chicken or Paper-wrapped Chicken. All are highly savoury though others may be moister; for example, Quick-fried Pepper Steak, Sliced Beef in Oyster Sauce, Quick-fried Diced Chicken in Soya Jam, Sliced Fish in Wine Sauce, Yunnan Ham in Honey Sauce, Quick-fried Pig's Liver with Tree Fungi, Sweet and Sour Pork, Giant Prawns in Shells Plain-fried with Garlic and Ginger, and Double-cooked Pork. Yet another alternative would be dishes in which meat is fried along with vegetables, such as Duck with Pineapple, Stuffed Red and Green Peppers, Stuffed Braised Mushrooms, Shrimps Quick-fried with Garden Peas, Beef Ribbons Quick-fried with Onions, Shredded Pork with Bean Shoots or Sliced Lamb Quick-fried with Spring Onions. The list can be prolonged indefinitely.

For elegance and daintiness, the wine-accompanying dishes are usually presented in small dishes (which are no larger than the side dishes used at a western dinner). The diners are meant to savour the food, not wolf it!

After the four light quick-fried wine-accompanying dishes comes soup followed by four 'heavy' dishes. The soup is intended to provide a breather in the procession of dishes.

The 'heavy' dishes called *Ta Ts'ai* should all be served, as a contrast, in very large bowls called *hai wan* (sea bowls) which are classified according to size as 'middle seas' and 'large seas' (or 'oceans'). Most of these will be soup type or braised dishes with lots of gravy, such as Shark's Fin, Bird's Nest, Sea-Cucumber, Eight Treasure Duck or Steamed Chicken, but there may be a roast, a Sucking Pig, Peking Duck or Pot-Roast Lamb, or a fish, which can be a Red Braised Whole Fish, or a Sweet and Sour Yellow River Carp.

This series of heavy dishes invariably ends with a sweet dish, more often than not sweet soup, perhaps Silver Ears in Crystal Syrup (silver ear is a tree-fungus), or one of the sweet soups made from lotus seeds, lotus roots, almonds, or water chestnuts.

In the Chinese cuisine the sweet dish does not conclude a meal but indicates the end of one series of dishes and the beginning of another. They provide a welcome pause and re-fresher in the long march of a Chinese banquet. Some of the sweet soup will be nothing more than warmed or chilled orange juice or cherry-coloured sweetened water, with a few small, sweet-filled dumplings floating in them.

After the *Ta Ts'ai* come four rice-accompanying dishes called *Fan Ts'ai* with a very plain soup. These dishes are meant to settle the stomach after the rich and savoury dishes which have gone before. With the arrival of the *Fan Ts'ai*, drinking, which is carried on between and during all the pre-vious courses, ceases.

In order to provide a contrast with the preceding quick-fried and heavy dishes, the rice-accompanying dishes aim at extreme simplicity. If *congee* (porridgy rice) is served, there should be at least two side dishes of salted or pickled foods to accompany it.

Among these plain rice-accompanying dishes, there would be a soup, vegetable dishes, and some plain meat dishes, or an assembled dish. Marrow Soup, Cabbage Soup Flavoured with Dried Shrimps, Plain Fried Spinach, Bamboo-shoots with Sze-chuan Pickled Cabbage, Mixed Vegetables with Fried Bean Curd, Shredded Pork Scrambled with Egg and Tree-fungi, Plain-fried Tile-piece Fish, or Tip-out Pickled Pork. If Peking Duck was served earlier, the carcase of the duck will have been simmered with plenty of cabbage to make a duck soup. Indeed, the duck soup is one of the classics of a ban-quet.

All the dishes in this final series are calculated to be in direct contrast to the elaborate dishes that have gone before, though sometimes one feels rusticity and plainness are carried to unnecessary extremes. Nevertheless gourmets and people who seem to make a profession of eating (and they abound in China!) will still make considerable inroads into the bowls of rice and vegetables even so late in the meal.

What I have described is quite an ordinary Chinese banquet or dinner of no great pretension. An official or mandarin banquet will be a lengthier and more elaborate affair. The correct procedure is to start with four light savouries, followed by four dried fruits, which are followed by four fresh fruits, followed by four crystallized fruits, and this before you even start on the cold dishes! When the heavy dishes are served, each should be accompanied by two to four small dishes, and the major sweet dish should also have its complementary small sweet dishes.

The heavy dishes and their accompaniments add up to over 20 individual dishes! Add the earlier savouries and fruits to the cold dishes and you have another 20! Apart from the small complementary dishes, there are also between-course sandwich dishes, which may be brought in with the wine-accompanying dishes as well as with the heavy dishes. In all, this gives a mimimum of more than 60 dishes!

I have personally experienced a banquet of this magnificence, but it pales beside the All-China Manchu Banquet in which the total number of dishes should be in the neighbourhood of 300!

In present-day China such senseless elaboration and wastefulness, although expressive of soaring human spirit, is regarded not only as archaic and feudal (which is a synonym of criminal), but downright counter-revolutionary. The evidence of several recipe books which I have collected from the People's Republic of China as well as conversations I have had with recent visitors to China, suggest that things have been brought very much down to earth. But the traditions of culinary excellence are deep-rooted, and the food in China is still excellent, but is more widely available and served in more sensible proportions with less fuss. The style of parties and official banquets in China is coming more into line with the normal good Chinese family meal.

Family Meal

What does a Chinese family meal consist of?

Briefly, a good Chinese family dinner is an abbreviation of a Chinese banquet. A family dinner for 6–10 people should consist of the rice-accompanying dishes of a banquet, one heavy dish, and a couple of quick-fried wine-accompanying dishes. Fish, fowl, meat and plenty of vegetables should balance one another. One or two salty dishes, which are always welcomed by rice-eaters, a meat soup and a plainer vegetable soup can also be served. All these dishes should be served simultaneously, although one or two quick-fried dishes which are best eaten very hot, can be brought in sizzling hot from the kitchen. Egg dishes appear frequently at a Chinese family meal, for there are millions of small farmyards scattered throughout China, and chickens, and consequently eggs, abound. Eggs frequently appear as Steamed Savoury Eggs, which is made of beaten egg mixed with meat broth and steamed. It can only be described as a custard-jelly, since it shimmers and shakes like a jelly but has the colour and consistency of custard. This dish goes very well with rice, and is often garnished with a spoonful of tangy chopped chives or spring onion, or, occasionally, with chopped ham, which is, of course, a luxury.

Eggs are sometimes scrambled with minced meat, mushrooms, onions, lard and some good broth. The dish is called Runny Yellow Egg (*Liu Huang Ts'ai*), and is another good runny dish to eat with rice.

Gravy Eggs are also common on the Chinese family dinner table. Hard-boiled eggs are simmered together with some meat in meat gravy, since they will then keep for days, can be cut into brown and yellow slices and served whenever required. The dish is often served up with the sliced cold-gravied meat which has been cooked in the same pot (the boiled eggs having been added only at the end). The so-called Egg Rolls, which are sometimes seen in Chinese restaurants abroad, consist of mixed meat stuffings spread on a layer of egg pancake, which is then rolled up like a Swiss Roll, and sliced into cross-sections. It is more elaborate than the previous dish, but not regarded by gourmets as nearly as satisfying. We Chinese only very occasionally make eggs into conventional omelettes, which can be cooked with all the varieties of stuffings imaginable. They are usually lightly stirred, rather than turned and folded as is normal in the West. The one thing which distinguishes a Chinese from a western omelette is the addition of wine or sherry, which seems to give it particular character. Seafoods, such as crabs, oysters and prawns are frequently cooked with eggs.

Classically, the term *fu-yung* should only apply to egg white and cornflour mixed with minced chicken (a completely white mixture). In the classical Peking dish Fu-Yung Sliced Chicken the mixture is slid spoonful by spoonful into hot oil, where it forms into slices which resemble thin white slices of chicken breast: hence the name.

Some cold broth is often added to the *fu-yung* mixture and it is then used as a white sauce in which other foods, particularly vegetables, are cooked to improve their taste. A well-known dish of this type is Fu-Yung Cauliflower. Indeed, almost all vegetables, even the hard ones like carrots, can be cooked as *fu-yung* dishes – but these must first be simmered in broth until tender before they are fried together with the *fu-yung* mixture. Fresh tender vegetables need only be fried separately in oil for a minute before the *fu-yung* is added and the two are fried together for another minute or so.

A Chinese meal is made up of many different dishes – ready-cooked ones, quick-cooking ones (such as quick-fried dishes), and slow-cooking ones, all of which are prepared at different times to be eaten together.

Most slow-cooking dishes are made in earthenware casseroles, which are a feature of Chinese homes. Both meat and fish are cooked in them. A chunk of fish, be it halibut, haddock or cod, is simply placed in a casserole, with half a pint of chicken broth, a few stalks of spring onion, a couple of slices of fresh ginger, 2 teaspoons of dried shrimps and two pieces of dried mushrooms, and left to simmer for 10–15 minutes with one or two tablespoonfuls of vinegar and wine, and the appropriate amount of seasonings. The resulting dish is delicious.

Most ready-cooked dishes, such as Gravy-Eggs, or jellied meats, can be sliced neatly and arranged on dishes in next to no time. Even cured, salted or wine-cooked poultry or white cut meat requires only to be cut or laid out neatly on a serving dish, and perhaps doused with some cold sauce or marinade.

All that quick-fried dishes require is a very short period of stir-frying over high heat with a couple of tablespoons of oil.

So, in spite of the considerable number of dishes which custom demands an efficient Chinese housewife can often serve a very respectable dinner in a matter of 30 minutes (if she has all the materials to hand). As long as she is in her own kitchen all the materials *will* be there! There is a characteristic lack of panic in the Chinese kitchen when suddenly confronted with half a dozen unexpected guests.

A housewife also can rely on warmed-up dishes in an emergency. Where typically, westerners consider such food not good enough for guests, there is a great range of dishes which are considered by the Chinese to be as good if not better warmed up, than in the original. Practically all the stewed and casserole dishes, and many assembled dishes can be warmed up. Sometimes a little fresh onion is fried in the oil, along with a little sauce and wine, and the reheated dish may well turn out better than when it was originally served, for the simple reason that, at the second go the chef can improve on or adjust the seasoning and sauces, remove any excess fat and generally perfect the dish.

One of the great favourites of home cooking in southern and coastal China is fried salt fish which some people serve with every meal. These salt fish have been dried thoroughly in the sun and have a strong taste of anchovy. They are fried in oil over low heat for 15–25 minutes (depending on the quantity). If you are not used to it, the smell of it frying is unbearable, but the delicious, crumbling, melting mouthfuls are considered infinitely superior to caviar. Because of its strong taste, salt fish is eaten with mouthfuls of plain boiled rice.

As a rice-accompanying dish, fried salt fish probably has no superior in the whole repertoire of Chinese cuisine. Since salt fish is inexpensive it is often considered poor man's food, but along with rice and plenty of vegetables (which are usually also cheap in agricultural countries) and soya bean products, such as bean curds, it provides a fairly well-balanced diet. This is exactly what Chinese peasants used to eat, and they were a strong hardy race. The Japanese, too, seemed to have survived on a similar diet. Even in these days of technological advance and comparative affluence in Japan, they still hanker after salt fish and bean curds, and various pickles, which, like the Chinese, they greatly prefer to the creamy delicacies of the West, both from the dietary, as well as from the culinary point of view. You will have to decide for yourself what the West can learn from the East when you have waded through this book!

Chinese Breakfast

Although the Chinese breakfast and the English breakfast of porridge (or cereal), bacon and egg, and tea or coffee, are worlds apart, there are, in fact, a good deal of underlying similarities. It would seem that each of the various breakfast foods has its special function; if it is salty and strong tasting it wakes up the muggy early morning palate; porridge, which is warm and filling, insulates one from the first chilly venture into the outside world in winter; fruit juice cleanses and refreshes the mouth; finally coffee, which is stimulating and aromatic, helps to awaken the sleepy human spirit to the prospects of the new day.

A Chinese breakfast also aims at helping in man's waking-up. The pickles, salted duck's eggs, and salt fish perform much the same function as the British bacon and egg. A big bowl of *congee* (soft watery rice) is almost the precise equivalent of British porridge. Roasted peanuts provide, like coffee, the heady aroma, and their nutty, rich crispness is in pleasing contrast to the soft rice. But the Chinese provide a wider range of breakfast foods than westerners. Thousand-Year-Old Egg (which, to be more precise, should be called Pickled Eggs) Meat Wool (a form of rich dehydrated meat, prepared by low-fire stir-frying), various jellied and pickled meats, and some smoked dishes – in fact, the majority of cold dishes from a banquet – can be incorporated into a Chinese breakfast. The main feature of the meal is that everything is cold, except the *congee*. The *congee* plays two roles: it is warming, like porridge, and refreshing, much as fruit juices are to westerners. Since there is no tradition of cold drinks in China, we have to content ourselves with the refreshing qualities of the watery rice. Actually Chinese much prefer this kind of refreshment to freezing cold drinks of which they are rather suspicious, much as they are always dubious of anything uncooked. Before the days of water purification, anything cold and un-cooked carried risk of contamination. Cold drinks were, until quite recently, quite alien to the Chinese palate.

There is one characteristic item eaten at Chinese break-fasts, which in a sense corresponds to cornflakes or cereals since it is best eaten dipped into *congee* or milk. In texture it resembles doughnuts (without being sugary). These *Yiu Tiao* (literally oil stick) are very much part and parcel of the Chinese way of life. They are made from a mixture of plain flour and self-raising flour, formed into two strips of dough twisted around one another like a cable rope. Deep fried in oil, the twisted cable rope rises and blows up to a light stick, about a foot long and an inch wide. It is eaten dipped in hot *congee*. Perhaps because of the absence of butter, the oil stick is a very important and integral part of the Chinese breakfast.

Unfortunately, a Chinese breakfast is not easily come by in the western world – hardly any Chinese restaurants are open for breakfast. In some ways it has the character of a Scan-dinavian spread: there are a number of dishes, several of them with the quality of pickled herrings (so popular with the Swedes and Norwegians) placed on the table in small plates and dishes. Although the Chinese breakfast is probably an acquired taste, it is worth trying, if only for a change, be-cause of its underlying parallels to the British breakfast. Those with catholic, rather than conservative tastes might enjoy the experience, and the meal is by no means unbalanced nutritionally.

Snacks and Tea-house Foods

The average westerner doesn't need to be gradually broken in to Chinese snacks and tea-house foods. In my experience anyone with a slight propensity for eastern and exotic food takes to them like the proverbial duck to water.

Chinese tea-house foods and snacks are not eaten with rice and so are seldom heavy or greasy. They are usually steamed rather than fried, and are brought to the table attractively arranged in multi-layered bamboo steam-baskets. When the baskets are lifted off one another, the steam from the food rises, giving off welcome and appetizing smells.

Most Chinese snacks would make excellent canapés, and add immense interest to cocktail parties; indeed, they might transform a cocktail party into a more food-conscious gathering, and create a new fashion in entertainment!

With the growth of Chinese communities abroad, Chinese snacks and tea-house foods can be found in restaurants where the Chinese themselves congregate. The Chinese community has to be large enough to make it worthwhile for the restaurateurs to produce them for daily consumption. Since most of the exiled Chinese in the West originate from Canton (or Kwangtung) where these foods abound, snacks and teahouse foods are available in many places in the China-towns of London, New York and San Francisco. They would mostly be far more popular if restaurateurs had made any attempt to introduce them to the western public, instead of reserving them for their Chinese customers.

Snacks and tea-house foods are very popular in China itself. There are no pubs or bars and most of the informal leisurely drinking takes place in tea-houses, where the savoury snacks take priority over alcohol, since, in any case, the customers are often drinking tea. Many Chinese of the leisure class used to spend a good deal of their time in these establishments. The selection of snacks to accompany wine, and light foods to satisfy the appetites of those wealthy cus-tomers who were indulging themselves, often exceeded the selection of alcoholic drinks and wine, which is very limited in China. The main categories of tea-house foods are as follows:

(1) NOODLES: fried or tossed in gravy, or in soup.

(2) STEAMED STUFFED-BUNS: different sizes, some with savoury meat stuffings, and some with sweet stuffings.

(3) SPRING ROLLS: some are fried, but the majority are stuffed with various fillings by the diners at the table.

(4) WRAPLINGS: consist of savoury meat stuffings wrapped in thin dough. They are either steamed, boiled or fried. There is a special category of these called *wuntuns* (made of extra thin dough).

(5) YUAN HSIAOS OR TANG YUANS: small sweet dumplings, usually served in soups.

(6) CONGEES: soft rice. In contrast to *congees* for breakfast which are served plain, *congees* in tea-houses are usually highly savoury.

(7) LOTUS LEAF WRAPPED SAVOURY RICE: usually consist of glutinous rice, steamed and wrapped in lotus leaves, with various savouries.

(8) FRIED RICE: numerous varieties.

(9) ASSORTED FRIED SAVOURIES: again there are many varieties; miniature fried crispy balls, fritters, pies, wraplings (the crispy *wuntuns*), *feng kuos* (olive-shaped, crumb-covered savouries), paper-wrapped foods.

(10) ASSORTED STEAMED SAVOURIES: including steamed 'bundles', *chang-fengs* (which are made from dough using rice flour stuffed and wrapped over like an omelette), miniature spare-ribs, etc.

(11) HSIAO MAIS: small open-topped bowl-shaped savouries made of dough formed into a bowl, and stuffed with savoury meat.

(12) CHINESE SWEETS AND DESSERTS: Sweet-stuffed dumplings and steamed buns (stuffed with sweetened bean paste), hot or chilled steamed fruits in syrup, varieties of sweet soups, sweet meats, fruit fritters, chilled crystallized fruits (used in Eight Precious Rice), are the favourite sweetmeats in China itself.

Chow Mein

Chow mein, or fried noodles, are a staple item of tea-house food. There are certain similarities in its preparation to Italian pastas, but there are probably many more Chinese *mein* (noodle) dishes than pastas. One of the reasons is that almost any quick-fried food can be used to garnish and add substance to *chow mein*. In coastal areas oysters are one of the principal ingredients of a noodle dish that resembles paella. Westerners are more used to eating their Chinese noodles fried (which are dry) than in soup or gravy, which is the usual practice in China. A bowl of gravy noodles often contains as much as ¼–½ lb. of noodles, apart from the other ingredients, and it is therefore very filling and warming in the winter.

Chinese fried noodles are first boiled and then fried in the strongly flavoured oil (or gravy) which is left in the frying-pan after shredded meats and vegetables have been fried. The noodles are fried until heated through and then the other ingredients are returned to the pan, except for a few pieces which are retained and re-fried for decoration. In a *chow mein* dish you can find shredded raw vegetables, cooked or dried vegetables (all of which have different textures), meat, seafoods (even prawns and abalone differ in texture), crisp noodles and crackling meat skin. It's a whole orchestra of taste and texture!

The one Chinese noodle dish which most nearly approximates to Italian pasta is tossed noodles, (a staple food of the North rather than the South), for the noodles used are boiled only and not fried. The sauces and shredded meat are mixed with the noodles at the table rather than by the chef in the kitchen (as is the case with fried noodles). The sauce is made from soya bean paste and minced meat, and resembles Bolognese sauce in appearance. The Chinese also add a great variety of raw vegetables, such as cucumber, radish, spring onions, coriander leaves etc., along with the soya and meat sauce, which add aroma and crunchiness to the dish.

The crispy noodles which are so popular in Chinese restaurants abroad are largely confined to Canton. In Canton they usually press the noodles against the flat bottom of the frying-pan, until they are slightly brown, then they are turned over like a pancake, and the soft top side is in turn pressed and fried to a similar crispness. As the Cantonese are inclined to use quite a lot of oil for this type of frying, people from other parts of China, especially from the North, often consider these Cantonese fried noodles too greasy. They would rather flavour the noodles by adding different ingredients, or vary the texture by combining crunchy shredded raw vegetables with crackling deep-fried foods, instead of making the crispy noodles even crisper. In fact crispy noodles are rare outside of Canton, but seem to have caught on in North America.

Spring Rolls (or Pancake Rolls)

The spring rolls served in restaurants or tea-houses in China are not necessarily deep-fried, as they usually are in Chinese restaurants in the West, but are more often soft pancakes which are spread out in front of each diner, who then chooses his own fillings from a whole variety of dishes of shredded foods laid out on the table, fills his individual pancake and rolls it up himself (turning in one end). The fillings are usually quick-fried, predominantly crunchy vegetables and shredded meats, with a selection of dried ingredients to provide the distinctive flavour. These fill-them-yourself pancakes are always a joy to make and eat.

The usual pancake rolls served in Chinese restaurants are good when freshly made, because the skin enclosing the crunchy vegetables and savoury meats is hot and crisp. The dough for Chinese pancakes should always be thin, and the filling crunchy, meaty and full of flavour. When the diner wraps his own pancakes, it is important that the fillings should be brought to the table freshly quick-fried, and the pancakes stuffed, rolled and eaten before they become cold and limp: crispness and crunchiness are the keynotes. As most of the best vegetables with these qualities are available in the spring, pancake rolls are most often served in that season, hence the evocative name 'spring rolls', as if all of spring were rolled up in them!

Wraplings or Chiao-tzu

Wraplings are called *Chaio-tzu* in China, and they come in various sizes. The most common ones have meat fillings wrapped in a thin dough, and measure about ¾ in. They are either boiled or steamed. The smaller ones wrapped in particularly large, thin dough-skins are sometimes called *wuntuns*, and may be fried to a crisp savoury. Translated literally *wuntun* means swallowing a cloud; indeed, well made *wuntuns* floating in clear soup resemble clouds.

In the north these wraplings are larger and more filling, and are sometimes eaten as a meal. They are occasionally fried very gently with just a film of oil on a flat-bottomed pan until the dough underneath has browned and slightly toasted. From time to time during cooking, the top of the wraplings are sprinkled with a mixture of water and vinegar to keep them moist. So while the meat fillings are cooked slowly inside, the top stays soft, the underneath crisp, and the inside meaty or juicy. These northern-style wraplings are called *kuo tiehs*, which means stuck to the pan. The favourite fillings for *kuo tiehs* are pork and lamb with plenty of leek, onion and some garlic. Seafood is never used. The northern Chinese, who prefer straightforward Peking food are inclined to be purists, and regard the use of seafood in wraplings as an adulteration!

On the other hand, the Cantonese can hardly make a move in the kitchen without introducing prawns, crabs and abalone. One of their favourite wraplings, called *hsiao mai*, has an open top. It is made by creasing the round rim of the dough (approximately 3 ins. diameter) as it is smoothed up round the filling which is placed in the centre. For decoration, a single shrimp or prawn is frequently put on top of each *hsiao mai*, before it is placed in a steamer for 20 minutes or so. Alternatively, a *hsiao mai* can be topped with a single small mushroom. Either way it makes an ideal canapé for a cocktail party.

Fried Rice

Fried rice has become a very popular dish in Chinese restaurants abroad, probably because of the constant demand among western customers for individual dishes that are complete in themselves. Another reason is that fried rice can be cooked from almost any kind or quantity of ingredients, so long as the eventual product is tasty, with egg and onion and one salty food (such as ham or bacon or salt beef) to contrast with the neutral blandness of rice. Mushrooms, peas, prawns, chicken or any other meat can be added to make fried rice more elaborate. Since these foods are in ready supply in most restaurants, fried rice is a convenience dish for both restaurateurs and western customers.

Good fried rice should of course be tasty, but primarily it should be light, dry and aromatic. It should never be messy and sloppy with gravy, for it is one of those dishes where, although many ingredients are mixed together, each of them should stand out distinctly: you should be able to see quite clearly the yellow of the egg, the green of the peas, the red of the bacon or ham, the pink of the prawns and the white of the rice. Good fried rice is in direct contrast to a savoury porridge. Because of its dryness, it is best eaten with a soup.

For a westerner dining alone, fried rice with one additional dish, such as Sweet and Sour Pork, Chicken Mushroom, Butterfly Prawns, Beef Ribbons and Onion, Spare Ribs, or Chopsuey makes an ideal meal, along with a bowl of soup or a glass of wine. One portion of fried rice is enough for two people along with two other dishes different in taste and texture.

Steamed Buns

Steamed buns which are called *pao-tzu* are popular in both north and south China. Their popularity is probably due to their convenience, as well as to the fact that they are practically self-contained meals. The savoury meat and vegetable stuffings, in their steamed raised-dough casing, are well flavoured as well as filling.

A little sugar is added to the dough and this tinge of sweetness often comes as a pleasant surprise to the westerner.

Since the gravy and meat are sealed within the bun, they are convenient for outdoor meals and picnics. A proportion of self-raising flour is used and the bun itself is quite light. One can get through quite a number of them, although 3 or 4 is enough for most people.

The stuffings for these buns vary widely – from roast pork to sweetened black or brown bean paste (which is the most widely used sweet ingredient in Chinese food, for it is also wholesome and satisfying). Some are even stuffed with meat jelly, which turns to gravy when the buns are steamed. These are called Soup Buns. A large amount of steam is always generated in rice cooking and steamed buns along with other steamed items can all be cooked conveniently together in the Chinese kitchen.

Yuan Hsiao

Yuan hsiao is a form of Chinese festival sweet, served in a rather bland rice soup. The sweet is round with a sweet core, and is about the size of a marble. It is made in rather an intriguing way. The solid sweet core – which may be a piece of crystallized fruit, or ground walnut mixed with sugar, chopped dates or sesame seeds mixed in molten sugar – is rolled on a tray of ground glutinous rice. After the core has picked up the ground rice from the tray, it is moistened with water and rolled again over a fresh spread of ground rice. This process is repeated until the core has become a perfectly round ball of the requisite size. The preparation of the *yuan hsiao* has become a festive game in China, much enjoyed by the family, especially the youngsters. When the *yuan hsiaos* are ready they are dropped into a pan of boiling water to simmer for 20–30 minutes (depending on their size and number). They are served 5–6 in a bowl, with Yuan Hsiao Soup, which is merely the water in which the *yuan hsiaos* have been cooked. This soup is refreshing because of its sheer blandness.

We Chinese love these *yuan hsiaos*, partly, I think, because of happy childhood memories of being allowed to do the rolling, and partly because a sweet dish with a light refreshing soup is always a pleasant contrast to an abundance of savoury food.

However, there is one danger in eating *yuan hsiaos*: the sweet core within can be many degrees hotter than the soup or the glutinous rice covering the outside. People have been known to pass out after swallowing a few in rapid succession, whether out of carelessness or sheer greed!

Soft Rice or Congee

Congee as we have seen is normally eaten at breakfast time in China. It can also be the equivalent of a soup and its methods of preparation are virtually infinite. There are a number of sweet *congees* (we Chinese are fond of sweet soups) but by far the majority are savoury.

One of the favourites is Gold and Silver Duck Congee, which is made by simmering rice for 1½ hours and then simmering a freshly killed chicken and a roast duck for a further 1½ hours in the *congee*, together with a small quantity of dried scallops. The *congee* is seasoned to taste. The meat is then stripped off the birds, added to the rice, and returned to the cooker for a very short period, perhaps with further adjustments in seasoning. Finally, the dish is sprinkled lightly with chopped chives and a drop or two of sesame oil. The white chicken meat represents the silver, and the brown duck meat the gold.

Chicken *congee* is cooked in precisely the same manner with the optional addition of a small amount of sliced abalone and dried mushrooms in the later stages.

Other favourite *congees* are Spare Rib Congee and Liver and Sliced Pork Congee. The meat for *congees* is generally first marinated in soya sauce, ginger and wine, and rubbed with a small amount of cornflour, before it is sliced and added to the simmering soft rice.

A very well known Cantonese dish is Sampan Congee, which could perhaps be described as Cantonese Chowder or soft rice paella, for various seafoods are added, together with some chicken, eggs and peanuts. As well as the clams, shrimps, prawns, crabs, lobsters and dried squid, which are essential, sliced ginger, garlic and chopped onion are basic ingredients. The resulting dish is such a gastronomic experience that once tasted it is never forgotten!

One of the best known of the sweet *congees* is La Pa Congee, a festive sweet which is always cooked and eaten, for some reason, on the 8 December (Lunar calendar). The number of ingredients used in this *congee* can vary from 8 to as many as 64. To name but a few, the following may be included: almond, walnut, lotus seeds, dates, melon seeds, raisins, gingko nuts, red beans, yellow beans, green peas and glutinous rice. The tougher ingredients are added first, and the more tender ones last. Sugar is added to the individual bowls only when the *congee* is served. This is a delicious dish which westerners should appreciate.

In general, to cook ordinary boiled rice, which is meant to be dry and flaky, approximately $1\frac{1}{2}$ times as much water as rice is used. To cook a *congee* the rice has to be cooked with not less than 12–15 times the amount of water. After washing the rice and bringing it to the boil in plenty of water, it should be left to simmer for 3–3½ hours. On its own it is a refreshing accompaniment to savoury foods. But this is perhaps an acquired taste, and may not appeal to the average westerner at the first trial. The savoury or sweet *congees* are in a different category, easily appreciated by a westerner. Unfortunately, *congees*, like the majority of Chinese snacks are usually available only in Chinatown restaurants, which cater principally to the Chinese community. They may take a little seeking out, and moreover, restaurant proprietors have a disconcerting habit of suggesting that you would be better satisfied if you went elsewhere – to the other 99 Chinese establishments which cater for the likes of you! But the Chinese understand the language of cash and patronage as well as anybody, and you should get what you want if you persist, or take a Chinese friend with you to explain your honourable intentions!

Lotus Leaf-wrapped Rice

This is another interesting item of Chinese seasonal snack food which is sometimes available in Chinatown restaurants. In China in the summer, when the lotus are in full bloom and plentiful, Lotus Leaf-wrapped Rice is a popular snack everywhere. The leaf is said to be more sweet-smelling than the flower itself, and the aroma of the leaf gives this snack its distinction.

The leaf is made into a parcel (oblong in shape and tied with string or reeds) and the rice, mixed with diced cooked chicken, ham, mushrooms and bamboo-shoots, is wrapped inside. Some of these ingredients are fried first and added to the boiled rice, and the others are folded into the rice with a small amount of gravy. Then they are all wrapped together in a large lotus leaf, measuring approximately a foot square.

The whole parcel weighs about ½ lb. These dark green parcels are then steamed for half an hour, when they are ready to be served.

They are usually piled up, 6–8 to a large serving dish, making quite an interesting sight when brought to the table; each person opens one on his own plate. The fragrant scent of the leaf which rises with the steam when the parcel is opened is one of the attractive features of Lotus Leaf-wrapped Rice. In Chinese it is called by the single word *chung*, which to every true-born Chinese has very nostalgic connotations.

Assorted Fried Savoury Crisps

These are deep-fried crisp savouries, such as small crisp prawn balls, meat balls, *wuntuns*, *feng kuos* (olive-shaped, crumbed savouries peculiar to Canton), various types of deep-fried foods, miniature spring rolls and pies.

Savoury crisps are made by frying morsels of foods till they are crisp and crackling. They may be seafoods, meat or fish which have been crumbed, coated in batter or placed on bread.

One very popular dish which is served nowadays in Pekinese restaurants abroad is Sesame Prawns. It is made very simply, but it is almost infallibly successful. Prawns are ground into a paste and a small amount of chopped pork fat is added. Chopped fresh fish can also be added, if necessary, for bulk. To bind them together a small amount of egg white and cornflour are beaten into the mixture. This paste is then spread thickly on to slices of bread with their crusts cut off, brushed with beaten egg and finally sprinkled thickly with sesame seeds. These slices of bread are then placed in wire baskets and lowered into boiling oil for 2–2½ minutes of deep-frying, until they are quite brown and crisp. They are then lifted out and thoroughly drained, and each piece is sliced into 6–8 fingers. The bread backing of these fingers is by then, very crisp, and with the thick savoury prawn spread and the aromatic sesame seeds, these Sesame Prawns are an unfailing delight to newcomer and connoisseur alike. Even when they are made without sesame seeds, and bread-crumbs are used instead, as is sometimes the case in the West, they are still invariably delicious. The top of each finger can be decorated with chopped chives or parsley, but it is not necessary.

Cantonese pies are made in the same manner as western pies, are about the size of mincepies, but are usually filled with pre-cooked diced ham, chicken, pork, mushrooms, prawns, etc. Because of this, and their smallness, they require no more than 15–20 minutes baking. Smaller ones are simply made by placing a good helping of filling in between two pieces of dough which are pressed together to seal the edges. These can either be deep-fried for 3–4 minutes or baked for 10–12 minutes. They are very similar to the deep-fried crispy *wuntuns* or miniature spring rolls.

Feng kuos, which are one of the goodies originating with the peasantry of Canton, are a type of fried food made in the shape of an olive, with a savoury filling of chopped roast pork, crab or prawn meat, mushrooms and bamboo shoots, flavoured with oyster sauce – all enclosed in a dough made of flour, cornflour and lotus-root flour and rolled in ground corn. Pieces of *feng kuo* which are about 2–3 ins. long are seldom deep-fried, but like fried bread, turned until they are brown all over. Once again, since there are so many variations and combinations of fillings, there is a great range of *feng kuos*. *Feng kuo* literally translated means Floured Fruit!

Crispy meat balls, prawn balls and fish balls are more common and can generally be found in Chinese restaurants abroad. The miniature *pao-tzu* (steamed buns with various fillings) are sometimes steamed first and finally fried until they are crisp, and served as crispy savouries.

While on the subject of deep-fried foods, paper-wrapped deep-fried dishes are probably peculiar to China. Paper-wrapped Chicken is a fairly familiar dish, which should be available from most restaurants, if you ask for it. What is most interesting about these dishes is the cooking method, rather than the foods used. Each bite-sized piece is cooked separately wrapped in a cellophane envelope. Different foods can be combined within each envelope provided that they harmonize in flavour. The only thing which the chef has to watch out for is that the envelopes are not fried too long, as the cellophane paper will brown and burn. In practice one should never fry them in very hot oil for longer than 4–5 minutes; one may have to let them cool down and then repeat the process a couple of times, a couple of minutes each time to ensure that the contents of the envelope are well cooked without the paper darkening.

The envelopes should, of course, be well drained before they are brought to the table, all piled up on a dish or even a silver salver. Each person helps himself to an envelope with a pair of chopsticks, and opens it by lifting the flap. The food inside, which has been temporarily insulated, will still be piping hot. What a boon this method of cooking is for those who like their food really hot, and what a thrill to discover how one envelope varies from another as they are opened in turn!

Assorted Steamed Savouries

There is another type of Chinese snack which is in a similar tradition and which also seems to be peculiar to China, the so-called Bundles. They consist mainly of strips of foods, such as ham, chicken, abalone or bamboo-shoots (foods which complement one another in flavour and texture and which can easily be cut into strips), which are wrapped in bean curd skins, or tied together in bundles with strips of fibrous vegetables, or even with chives or stalks of spring onion. The different constituents can either be first cooked or marinated separately (those which are tougher should be cooked, tender ones need only be marinated) and then, after they have been made into bundles and tied together, they are sealed and steamed for 10–15 minutes. Foods of different type, texture and colour can all be tied together in decorative bundles and arranged on the serving dish like so many steaming miniature Christmas crackers! In Chinese tea-houses, the bundles are usually steamed in small bamboo baskets (6–8 ins. in diameter), which hold dishes little more than half their size, each containing two or three bundles – an elegant and dainty sight.

Almost any dish, particularly the quick-fried ones which consist of chopped food, can be made in a miniature version, steamed in a basket steamer and presented in this dainty manner. A typical dish of this type and size is Miniature Spare Ribs, which have been chopped to ½ in. lengths and fried with a small amount of fermented black beans and chilli oil, or chicken pieces chopped to a similar size and fried with sliced ginger, black beans, onion and garlic. After about 2 minutes frying over high heat, they are neatly arranged in small heatproof dishes, placed in small basket steamers, and steamed for 10–12 minutes to tenderize them. Chinese salted sausage which looks like a miniature salami is frequently cooked and presented in this manner. These miniature dishes are reasonably inexpensive; at a tea-house lunch one can have a whole array of small dishes which were originally brought to the table piled to a great height in layers of baskets, almost like a lunar rocket with detachable sections!

Other foods which I have often seen and eaten prepared in

this manner are Quick-fried or Braised Sliced Pork Liver with Wood Ears, Braised Chicken Giblets and Quick-fried Sliced Kidney in Hot Soya Sauce (with chilli). All these dishes are miniatures, steamed and served on heatproof plates smaller than ordinary saucers. Apart from the elegance of such small portions, they are just right to be savoured and nibbled between sips of wine or tea during the ebb and flow of conversation. For this is exactly how the Chinese bourgeoisie pass a leisurely afternoon – eat a bit, talk a bit, and, occasionally, a refreshing sip or nibble.

Sweets and Desserts

These are yet another snack served in Chinese tea-houses for leisurely consumption. Chinese sweets are not outstanding by western standards, but they have their merits. However, they are rare in Chinese restaurants, except for the perennial lichee (or even lichee and ice-cream!). This is probably because it is not the normal Chinese tradition to serve sweets at meal times, and partly because they are finicky to make in restaurants where they are already very busy. Also, in contrast to savoury foods, Chinese sweets do not really compare with western sweets.

As we have already seen, Chinese restaurants seldom go in for lengthy cooking, and rely mainly on stir-frying even for their savoury dishes. Sweet dishes all take time to prepare, usually require different pots and pans which may be difficult to obtain abroad. Moreover the majority of the amateur instant chefs who practise abroad, have not had the opportunity to serve an apprenticeship in sweets. Even in China the kitchens are almost always engaged with savouries, and sweets and desserts are either neglected and dropped altogether from restaurant menus or replaced by western sweets. It might be mentioned, *en passant*, that Fortune

Cookies, like Chopsuey, its savoury counterpart, is not a Chinese sweet at all! It is an American invention.

The one Chinese sweet which appears to have caught on recently in Pekinese restaurants abroad, is Glaced Apple (often indiscriminately called Toffee Apple, confusing it with the sweets sold to children on fair grounds). The more precise term for the true Pekinese dessert is Drawn Thread Apple, a name which refers to the thin threads of molten sugar which form as the pieces of apple are taken from the pan. This dish is interesting for the unique way in which apple is served. The fruit is first cored, peeled and chopped into 6–8 pieces. They are battered with egg and flour and deep-fried for 3–4 minutes. At the same time some brown sugar is heated in a saucepan with a reasonable amount of oil until the sugar has completely melted (some honey may be added to this syrup). The deep-fried pieces of apple are then put into the saucepan and turned in the syrup, until the surface of every piece is completely covered.

Then the apples are removed from the pan, placed in a warmed, greased bowl and brought quickly to the table, where, as they are pulled apart with chopsticks, the molten sugar is drawn into long threads, like threads of molten glass. The apples are then plunged individually into a large crystal bowl of iced water. With the sudden impact of the water the threads of sugar harden into needles, and the syrup covering the apples into a shining brittle glaze, which cracks readily when it is bitten into. The sensation is like the cracking of thin ice on a pond at the onset of winter. In more elaborate versions, sesame seeds are sprinkled over the sticky, molten sugar on the apples before they are plunged into water.

Two other Chinese sweets which have made occasional appearances abroad are Almond Tea and Almond Junket. The former is made simply by mixing finely ground almonds with finely ground rice and boiling them together in water and sugar, stirring continuously so that the sediment does not stick to the pan. The 'tea' is ready after some 15–20 minutes of simmering and stirring. It can be drunk hot or cold. Almond Tea is typical of a certain kind of Chinese dessert which is prepared and served in soup or tea form. There are numerous varieties, many of which resemble orange juice or cherry juice, often with some small sweet-cored *yuan hsiao* balls served in them. The soup or tea is usually filtered and re-filtered until it is crystal clear. For westerners all these 'teas' and 'soups' are far better served well chilled simply because it is not in the western tradition to drink sweet liquids hot.

Almond Tea is made into Almond Junket by adding agar-agar or gelatine. It is usually sliced into triangular or other shapes, and served in sweetened or honeyed water. Chilled in the refrigerator it is most refreshing on a hot summer day.

The best known of Chinese party or banquet sweets is Eight Jewel Rice, which is a kind of rice pudding, similar to Christmas pudding. It is a steamed rice pudding studded with many coloured fruits, and turned out of a mould (bowl). The rice used is always the glutinous variety, with layers of puréed sweetened red beans and chopped dates interspersed in layers. The fruits and nuts most usual in this dish are dates, raisins, prunes, candied cherries, ginger, orange peel, almonds, chestnuts, walnuts, ginko nuts, dried lichees, dried dragon-eyes, water melon seeds, lotus seeds, etc. Imaginatively made and well cooked it is a splendid and colourful pudding. Like Christmas pudding it improves if a glass of heated liqueur is poured over it and set alight.

Another series of Chinese sweets are steamed fruits with honey syrups. Almost any large fruit suitable for steaming can be made into this type of sweet. One of the most popular and best known is Steamed Pears in Honeyed Syrup. The pears are peeled (but the stalk retained), just covered with water and simmered. After 45 minutes the water will have reduced by half. Sugar is added (and some honey if desired), and the fruits simmered for another 10 minutes. The pears are removed and arranged in a large deep bowl, and the honeyed liquid is poured over them. The dish is chilled and served. In more elaborate versions the pears, or other fruits, are painted with different coloured syrup to which a little liqueur has been added. The beauty of the dish depends upon peeling the pears carefully and leaving the stalks absolutely firm and intact, as if the fruits were still hanging from a tree. (If there are leaves attached to the stem they should be left on.) Each person is served with a whole pear and a good spoonful of syrup. The sweet, chilled fruit is pleasant after or during a hot Chinese meal.

Peking Dust is a well-known sweet which is not actually indigenous. It was invented by the western colony in Peking in the 1920s for its own consumption. It consists principally of light, powdered chestnut, piled up in a mound and topped with a large blob of cream.

A truly indigenous sweet from Peking is Ice-Mountain Fruit Salad, which simply consists of slices of a half a dozen different types of fresh fruit peeled and laid on a bed of chipped ice. The ice can, of course, be built up into a miniature mountain and the pieces of fruit piled over it. In Peking, we used to dip each piece of fruit in a saucer of sugar before eating it. So when this sweet is served, a few saucers of sugar are placed strategically around the table. The Chinese seem to eat more dips than most westerners, using them to accompany savouries as well as sweets. Sliced lotus root is a frequent ingredient in these mixed fruit dishes; it has a very crunchy texture, but is seldom used in the West.

There are a whole series of fritters which are very similar to their western counterparts. Sliced fruits are coated in a batter of egg and flour, fried in oil (or butter) and sprinkled with sugar. Simple as they are, they are very satisfying. They can be made with apples, bananas, or even with potatoes, or sweet-potatoes in China.

A much more peculiarly Chinese sweet is Sweet Wuntuns – *wuntuns* stuffed with sweetened bean paste and then deep-fried to make them crisp. They can be eaten sprinkled with sugar, or with honeyed syrup.

Many of the sweets which are served in Chinese tea-houses are in fact sweetmeats, a term which was in common use in England a century or so ago to describe a variety of confections. Chinese sweetmeats are made largely from bean paste, chopped dates, water chestnut flour, lotus root flour, ground lotus seeds and cornflour, mixed with sugar and then steamed. They are served cut into slices or slabs.

For example, the sweetmeat made from water chestnut flour is a transparent slab, with streaky layers of fresh water chestnut embedded in it. It is intriguingly rubbery and crunchy. Most other sweetmeats have a firm, rubbery, jelly-like texture, and are interesting either for their distinctive flavour – such as that of lotus seeds or brown or black bean paste – or for the contrast they provide to the other savoury dishes. In Chinese tea-houses, where people sit and nibble at morsels of foods and variety, rather than quantity or ostentation, is the keynote, there is normally available a range of sweets not usually obtainable from the average restaurant unless ordered in advance. The same is true of Chinese restaurants abroad. Chinese desserts and sweetmeats can only be found in Chinatown restaurants, which are the equivalent of Chinese tea-houses catering to the Chinese community until late into the night; the customers sit over their tea or wine, and can do so for as long as they want. Otherwise, the sweets and desserts available in the average Chinese restaurants abroad are quite dismal.

PART TWO

Chinese Food Abroad

Ninety-nine per cent of the readers of this book are likely to encounter Chinese food abroad, so that is what we will deal with first.

Everything suffers a sea change when removed from its native shores. Chinese food and cooking are naturally no exception. Some changes are for the better, but, in the case of Chinese food abroad, the changes seem either to be for the worse or to involve a loss of authenticity.

In America and Canada Chinese food seems to be represented (or mis-represented) by chopsuey; in the North of England by sweet and sour pork and fried Pacific prawns with chips; and on both sides of the Atlantic by Barbecued Spare Ribs, which in size and length are more Texan than Chinese. In China, pork spare ribs are seldom more than ½ in.– ¾ in. long. The whole piece is put into the mouth, and by a well-practised motion of the tongue, teeth and mouth, the bone is stripped of its meat.

On the European continent, especially in France, Chinese food has to compete with stronger national cooking traditions and Chinese food there has maintained its own individuality and the restaurants are less like conveyor-belts. But in Northern Europe, where Chinese food is more widespread and popular than in the poorer Latin countries, the general tendencies are similar to those of Britain and America, inclining towards great care in presentation without corresponding accuracy of reproduction and authenticity in flavour, which in China we always consider most important.

The general change suffered by Chinese food and cooking when it comes abroad can be attributed to two causes: first, the lack of taste and background knowledge on the part of most customers, which allows cooks and restaurateurs to take liberties which would be unacceptable to Chinese customers. Secondly, the need for restaurants, especially the more popular and prosperous ones, to adopt production-line methods. The need to adapt to local materials is only marginally to blame. Most of the materials used to cook in China are identical to those in common use here; indeed, in many cases the materials which are available in the West are superior (such as beef, lamb and eggs). And as for Chinese ingredients and flavourings, most are imported these days. A few of the fresh vegetables and fish which are popular in China may be difficult or impossible to obtain in the West, but these would only affect a few dishes.

Since most of the foods required are generally available, those Chinese restaurants which cater principally for the Chinese communities can usually produce dishes approximating very nearly to traditional Chinese specialities. On the other hand, those whose clientele consists largely of westerners do not always maintain traditional standards. Proprietors may feel they 'know what the customer wants' and provide a series of popular, inoffensive but uninteresting dishes, and in this way keep their restaurants full.

In some ways, perhaps the local cooks and proprietors are right, for, after all, most Chinese food in the West is eaten not by fastidious connoisseurs, but by the population at large, who, originally, were simply not adequately catered for. There were few places to eat at a reasonable price after 6 p.m.; the choice was virtually between fish and chip shops and expensive hotels, and people wanted a sit-down meal with their family in a reasonably clean place which would not bankrupt them. The principal function of Chinese restaurants nowadays is to provide hot savoury food in reasonable quantities; they know that as long as they are able to do this they will never go out of business. The good basic anchor dishes will always be in demand.

Basic Dishes of Chinese Restaurants Abroad

The following are the most popular dishes served in Chinese restaurants in the West:

Chopsuey
Chow Mein
Fried Rice
Sweet and Sour Pork
Cha Shao Pork (Cantonese roast pork)
Spare Ribs
Chicken and Almond
Chicken with Mushrooms
Pancake Roll
Egg Fu-yung
Fried Pacific Prawns in Batter
Shrimps in Tomato Sauce
Duck with Pineapple
Crispy Meat Balls
Shredded Beef with Onion
Sliced Pork with Vegetables
Shrimps, Abalone and Peas
Sliced Meat and Vegetable Soup
Egg Drop Soup
Fish Ball Soup
Wuntun Soup
Crab and Sweet Corn Soup
Fried Mixed Vegetables
Chow Chow
Lichees

Although this collection would not make an All-China Imperial Mandarin Banquet, it does not deserve the disdain and distaste with which it is sometimes regarded by would-be connoisseurs. Only a few are without pedigree, and although they have all suffered a slight sea change, they are still recognizable, and, if properly prepared, wholesome and tasty; they can still make a hungry mouth water. It depends on how well they are cooked. If one wishes to jeer at these basic 'anchor' dishes one should also remember that they are responsible for a turnover of one billion dollars in the western world every year!

Anybody who is interested in food might ponder upon the secret behind these dishes; and chefs newly arrived from the east cannot afford to ignore them either.

If a chef were to put some of the authentic Chinese classical or regional dishes on the menu with their unfamiliar names, they would probably not be ordered for several days, because of the customers' disinclination to experiment with their stomachs and good money. In due course, the food will either have to be thrown away, or chopped up and combined with the other mish-mash dishes for which there is always a regular demand. So the pressure on the new chef to conform is great. The proprietors and the other cooks whose policy is based on well-tried experience, are at least as conservative as the customers. As for the customers, they need educating. But Chinese chefs and restaurateurs are not in the West to educate, they are here merely to make a living. So change comes only very slowly and imperceptibly. Yet change there has been.

The origin of any change can be traced to the nostalgia of the Chinese for the authentic food which they so enjoyed in China. This nostalgia can only be satisfied when vision and circumstance meet.

To serve good authentic Chinese food in restaurants requires not only attention to service, presentation and publicity. It also requires a different managerial attitude: a degree of vision, organization, and steadfastness of purpose. Wherever these back the venture, the proprietors have almost invariably been rewarded with success, as is seen from the current popularity and success of Peking restaurants which are streets ahead of the Chinese restaurants serving basic dishes. Many of these restaurants have grown from humble origins, often situated in the outer suburbs or even in remote slums. Here in London, outposts like Wembley, Mitcham and Willesden have given rise to restaurants whose subsequent progress has been steady and unimpeded.

The genuine Cantonese (southern school) restaurants have had a different history. They were originally Chinese eating joints, which catered for the local Chinese seamen and labourers at the docks in the East End of London (just as they did in San Francisco), and dated back to the First World War in London and to the middle of the last century in California. In London they originated in Limehouse and have now arrived in the City under the very eaves of St Paul's Cathedral. They serve good-class Cantonese food. In the U.S.A. Chinese food of sorts has spread through the fifty states, but authentic Cantonese food is seldom found outside Chinatown.

At the same time another significant change has been taking place, which should have an important bearing on the trend of Chinese catering in this country and the rest of the western world. Throughout western Europe during the past fifteen years there has been an increase in the Chinese population – itself principally engaged in the food business – which expects a reasonably high standard in the establishments which cater for it. The present Chinese population in Europe is at least ten times larger than the former Chinese population of seamen and labourers who were the original customers of Chinese restaurants in the West. As western customers acquire an improved palate and more educated taste, the turnover of these Chinese restaurants which serve authentic foods will rise, and the chances of failure on the part of those Chinese establishments which doggedly adhere to conventional mish-mash will increase. So the day when good standard Chinese food will be the rule rather than the exception may be nearer than we dare to hope.

There will always be some Chinese dishes which are intrinsically good but which restaurants will find difficulty in serving regularly. Chinese restaurants are up against problems common to all restaurants: lack of time and space, and shortage of hands. That is why one so seldom comes across any of the numerous long-cooked dishes, which are so basic to Chinese home cooking; dishes which require long simmering, or prolonged steaming, or lengthy multi-phase cooking and marinating – such a change from the usual quick-fried offerings. What connoisseurs miss most are the tip-out meat puddings, earthen-pot Chinese casseroles, long-simmered red-cooked dishes and steamed multi-phase-seasoned poultry, which are all typical and characteristic of a good Chinese meal: or the jellied or drunken or smoked meats, and the exquisitely marinated thin-sliced vegetables, which are by no means only great banquet dishes. However, if you want to try out a Chinese restaurant, choose a simple single dish, such as chow mein or fried rice. It may turn out quite reasonable; for some establishments, though very poor at pretentious dishes, are excellent at basic ones.

If you are only interested in the most authentic Chinese foods, served specifically to the Chinese community, gravitate towards Chinatown (or any area where the Chinese community gathers) and ask the first Chinese you meet who appears to be fully awake, where you can get good real Chinese food. The place is usually either just around the corner or right in front of your very eyes.

For the majority of people, however, the problem is how to make the best of the dishes on the menu in a basic Chinese restaurant. Let us take a look at Chinese restaurants from the outside. Some have been modernized, but the majority are slightly dingy and unprepossessing (as many restaurants appear in broad daylight, especially in the morning). But do not let outward appearance put you off, they may have more warmth and charm to offer than you suspect! Occasionally you may come across an establishment which is polished and glittering with plate glass and lacquered eaves. But feel the thickness of your wallet before you enter, or at least take a good look at its menu first, and examine the prices of the individual dishes. If the prices are reasonable go in by all means, for even if the food is not above average, at least the environment will be.

You should take a good look at the menu in a Chinese restaurant before you make your selection, although they all seem to have the same main divisions: Soups, Chopsueys, Fried Rice, Noodles, Meats, Poultry, Fish and Seafoods, Vegetables, Sweets and Desserts. The problem which immediately arises is not so much *which* dishes to choose, but *what combination*. The first thing to remember about a Chinese meal is that it is supposed to be communal. Although each person should be consulted about his likes and dislikes, you should aim at a balanced selection for the whole party at the table. It is up to the host or hostess to make the final choice, not the individual.

It is normal to have at least three dishes and a soup for a Chinese meal; so two or three is the minimum number to make the meal worthwhile, and the more the merrier. It is customary to have at least one more dish than there are people: the ideal number of diners is six, with a selection of seven or eight dishes, in addition to soup.

If you are dining alone, and all you want is a tasty and

filling meal at not too great a cost, choose a soup, and one of those self-contained composite dishes of rice or noodles with meat and vegetables on top, which are so popular in Chinese restaurants. If you are still hungry order a spring roll or pancake roll as well. This meal should not cost more than about 60p in England, and two dollars in the U.S.A. If you are exceptionally hungry, my advice would be fried rice (special or otherwise), and one of the following dishes: Chopsuey, Sweet and Sour Pork, Chicken and Almond (or Mushroom), Beef and Pimento (or Onion), Crispy Meat Balls, all washed down with a soup (any soup). The meal can be concluded with coffee or tea.

For two, along with one of the above, order one more meat or fish dish, and a vegetable dish. You then share three dishes (meat, fish, vegetables), fried rice (supplemented with boiled rice if necessary), and soup for two.

If you are in a party of three or four, all you need do is add one more dish – duck, egg, or seafood – to the previous selection, giving four dishes, a double portion of fried rice (and/ or boiled rice) and soups. Apart from rice and soup, for the sake of variety you should never order a double portion of any of the other dishes; indeed you should raise your index finger to emphasize one portion, and it is a wise precaution to mention the price which goes with it so that the waiter can never claim that he brought double portions; these are, in any case, often only marginally larger than single portions. A second round of the dishes which have been enjoyed most can then be ordered.

If you are in a party of five or six persons, you should have, in addition to the basic dishes, both the duck and egg (*fu-yung*) dishes, and ask as well for a Sliced Steak in Oyster Sauce, which may or may not be on the menu, but which any self-respecting Chinese restaurant should be able to produce on the spot. If the restaurant cannot produce the dish, or is not prepared to oblige, it is time for you to withdraw your custom (at least inform the management of your intention). Sliced Steak in Oyster Sauce is a sure test of a restaurant: whether the proprietors are buying decent beef (which is expensive), whether the chef knows his job, and whether the management is obliging. Since there is now such a good choice of Chinese restaurants, and five or six customers are not entirely inconsequential, the waiters and management should be made to feel they have to pull their socks up if they wish to stay in business. However inscrutable we Chinese may look to the European, we are acutely aware of competition (particularly of the Chinese restaurant around the corner!). So the threat of taking your custom elsewhere would be taken seriously.

Soups and Vegetables

For your vegetable dish a simple, straightforward dish, such as Fried Spinach, Fried Greens, Fried Bean Sprouts, Fried Pea Pods, or Fried Cauliflower is usually best (*but not* Mixed Vegetables). Mixed vegetables, being the most popular and common in Chinese restaurants, are likely to be pre-cooked and left to stand to await orders and may be limp and no longer fresh. The other vegetable dishes have to be cooked specially and individually, and are usually fresh, crisp and crunchy. Freshly fried vegetables are often among the best dishes available even in high-quality Chinese restaurants, with menus of over a hundred dishes.

As for soups in basic Chinese restaurants, the fact is that one soup is much the same as another; they are very likely to have been prepared from the same broth. This, in a way, simplifies the diner's problem; if you want a soup you can settle on any one of them, so long as its name appeals to you! Fortunately, the majority of Chinese soups, even though prepared by unsophisticated chefs, are clear soups and reasonably tasty. My experience in basic restaurants is that, whether the soup is Fish Ball, Wuntun, Egg-drop, Sliced Meat and Watercress, or Crab and Sweet-Corn, they are all value for money, so long as they are hot, which you must insist upon.

In general, it is often good practice to leave the waiter or manager to recommend at least one or two choices, since, after all, he should know what there is in the kitchen, what is freshest, and whether the chef is in a good mood or not for preparing certain dishes. Make your own choice first, and then leave the waiter or manager to fill in the gap, rather than the reverse.

Boiled Rice and Fried Rice

Without going into the subtlety of flavours, or delicacy of texture, I think the chief attraction of Chinese food to westerners is that it is varied, tasty and savoury without being overpowering. It takes wide experience of Chinese food to fully appreciate nuances in flavour and texture, so fried rice, which is tastier and more savoury than boiled rice, is better for the average westerner. Boiled rice is better with a large selection of dishes, for its neutrality combines more equably with other dishes of individual character than fried rice. Actually, the Chinese look upon fried rice as a snack-dish made of left-overs to be eaten at home. It is hardly ever seen in a restaurant in China.

Yet well-cooked fried rice can be very appetizing. It should be dry and aromatic, and is delicious with soup, but even better with an additional dish – whether meat and vegetables, fish or seafood.

If one does not wish to stretch to an extra dish, which may cost more than fried rice itself, a good adjunct to the rice and soup is a Spring Roll (or Pancake Roll). A Spring Roll is crisp and has a savoury filling, is easily acceptable to the average western palate, and seldom costs more than a quarter of an average meat dish. Spring Rolls are, by the way, also a good choice for children to whom Chinese food may be a little strange.

When you are choosing for a party of more than three, the guiding principle is variety: variety in type of food, in colour and in cooking methods, bearing in mind, of course, individual preferences. In other words, a balanced and interesting menu, with something for everyone. For instance, if one person likes beef, another pork, and another duck, and still another egg and prawns, your choice could be: Sliced Beef in Oyster Sauce, Sweet and Sour Pork, Barbecued Spare Ribs, Cantonese Orange Duck, Chicken and Mushroom, Prawn Fu-Yung and Deep-fried Butterfly Prawns.

If one person does not like a certain dish, there are always others which will be acceptable. Occasionally you may have a vegetarian among you, but Chinese restaurants (unless they are too rushed) can usually produce a vegetarian dish or two, if coaxed.

My own experience is that with a young party, if you order only one dish more than there are people, whatever you order the plates will be swept clean, and you will probably have to call for more.

Ordering extra dishes is very much in the Chinese tradition. It happens in China all the time, at home as well as in restaurants. Whenever dishes or courses seem to be running out and everyone is still eating enthusiastically, the shout of *Tien Ts'ai!* goes up, and more dishes will at once be concocted in the kitchen. These hot, freshly cooked dishes are brought to the table when all the other food has disappeared, and are attacked eagerly. A good host is always alert and he shouts for the extras with pride.

To introduce someone to Chinese food, a good, safe, tempting selection might be a dish of Spare Ribs to start with (and urge him to use his fingers), Shredded Beef and Onion, Chicken Mushroom, Sweet and Sour Pork, Prawn Fu-yung, Pancake Roll (don't call it Spring Roll, the word 'pancake' is more reassuring). There is little here to object to, especially if he is hungry (which is the only right time to introduce anybody to a new type of food). Once he is initiated, and begins to feel at home with Chinese food there should be no stopping him.

In China, and occasionally even in Chinese restaurants abroad, the normal practice is for the customer to name the price he is prepared to pay for a table of party or banquet food. Say it is agreed that you wish to spend $60 or £15, only then do you begin to discuss the dishes you would like with the proprietor; he will call in the chef for support, and provide you with information about the market and seasonal produce. A westerner might be surprised that the number of people in the party would not be mentioned at all. It would be taken for granted that twelve or fifteen dishes or courses were required, sufficient or more than sufficient for a party of anything from eight to a dozen people. Indeed, it would be quite out of place for the restaurateur to specify that the food would only be sufficient for eight or ten people. He would lose business immediately and be shunned by his Chinese customers for calculating his margin so fine. Any mention of the number of people per table, and reflections on the quantity of food to go round, would immediately suggest meanness of spirit and purse, instead of largesse and style. A dinner-party is better not given at all than given with its style cramped.

At the time of writing, one should be able to obtain a good table of banquet food – ten to twelve courses, sufficient for at least ten people – for $60–$80 in New York and £15–£20 in

London; except of course if you are more interested in fashion than food. In more trendy places you can easily be charged double these amounts. But for show rather than good cuisine there are better places than Chinese restaurants.

Getting to know Chinese Dishes

If you have a genuine interest in food and Chinese food in particular, your problems are principally how to judge, appreciate (and if necessary cook), the anchor dishes which make up the menus of over 95% of all Chinese restaurants abroad. There is nothing like trying your hand at cooking these few basic dishes; once you have done this your knowledge will be so firmly based that you will always be one up on your friends or even the restaurateurs. Besides, you might become a successful restaurateur yourself!

You will also want to become more knowledgeable about the traditional and regional ramifications of Chinese food. Unfortunately, authentic, classical dishes of China are only normally available from some 10% of the Chinese restaurants abroad (although the majority can cook and serve them if pressed or bribed to do so). So how can you get to know and appreciate them and perhaps even cook them yourself? Once you are prepared to try this, you will find that whatever the Chinese can do, you can do just as well with a little practice and experience. There is less to the mystique of Chinese food and its preparation than you might imagine and there is nothing you cannot master as long as you are interested.

We shall start with the basic dishes as served in most restaurants. Although many of these are criticized for being westernized, anglicized or even bastardized, most are still recognizable as Chinese. I shall limit myself to only a score or so of these which are served in all Chinese establishments throughout the western world, giving a thorough description, and a detailed and well tried recipe for each. This should help you to feel more at ease in restaurants, or to reproduce them at home. Using these basic dishes, many more can be produced simply by following the same procedure but changing some of the ingredients.

Chopsuey

One of the most renowned of the anchor dishes is chopsuey with all its variations. The largest selection I have seen on a single menu is twenty-one, which is probably twenty too many – since, basically, they are really all the same thing. Chopsuey consists mainly of bean sprouts and other shredded vegetables, cooked with shredded quick-fried meat of one sort or another and sometimes flavoured with a few prawns and shrimps, with lots of gravy at the bottom of the dish and capped with a thin omelette. What can be more savoury and mouth-watering if you are really hungry?

The distinctive character of chopsuey comes from the fresh and crunchy bean sprouts combining with the savoury meat and gravy. Bean sprouts must not be confused with bamboo-shoots (which in their thrusting native state can measure over 1½ ft in length and 4 ins. in diameter). Bean sprouts are the same as bean shoots, produced by spreading Mung beans between damp cloths or blankets. After a couple of days they will start to sprout, and after about five days the sprouts will have grown to several times the size of the original beans and be ready to be separated from the husks for use in cooking. As you can imagine, bean sprouts are cheap; a large handful of beans can produce a quarter of a bucket of sprouts and Chinese restaurants tend to use them liberally.

Fresh bean sprouts are sweet and extremely crunchy, and require only minimal frying. They are a most versatile food for they can be combined with almost any meat or vegetable.

Tomato is a common ingredient, and tomato sauce is added along with soya sauce and the other regular constituents of the sauce when the shredded meats are being fried. The resultant gravy, in which the bean sprouts are tossed and turned, has a familiar taste to the western palate (that of ketchup), but it has Chinese overtones.

Chopsuey has two characteristics of Chinese cooking: savouriness and crunchiness, with two familiar ingredients of the West, tomato and egg. Probably it is this blend of the exotic with the familiar which accounts for its popularity.

On the other hand, chopsuey is the antithesis of real Chinese culinary art, which requires that flavours are kept distinct, and not jumbled, however savoury the result; and chopsuey is really no more than a savoury mess!

At its worst, the bean sprouts in chopsuey are stale and limp, or in some cases, for lack of enough bean sprouts, shredded cabbage is added, along with shredded meat which may also be stale and indeterminate, and there is far too much tomato sauce. The result is a dish not only quite alien to any Chinese tradition, but to any concept of good food.

CHOPSUEY   (for 5–6 people with other dishes)

1 egg
4 tablespoons vegetable oil
4 oz. meat (pork, chicken, lamb or beef)
2 tablespoons soya sauce
1 teaspoon salt
1½ teaspoons sugar
2 tablespoons dry sherry
1 tablespoon tomato sauce (or purée)
4 tablespoons chicken broth
dash of pepper
2 tablespoons lard
4 spring onions (cut in 2 in. segments)

1 clove garlic (crushed)
1 slice root ginger (finely chopped)
¾ lb. bean sprouts
½ teaspoon M.S.G. (or ½ chicken stock cube)

Beat egg and make a thin omelette in a small omelette pan in 2 tablespoons of oil, and put aside.

Slice the meat thinly and then into matchstick strips. Fry in 2 tablespoons oil for 2 minutes over high heat. Add sugar, soya sauce, tomato sauce and half the sherry. Continue to stir-fry for half a minute. Add chicken broth and pepper. Heat until the mixture boils. Stir gently for ½ minute and withdraw from fire.

Heat lard in a saucepan. When it has melted, add spring onion and crushed garlic and ginger. Stir-fry for ½ minute over high heat. Add bean sprouts and sprinkle with salt. Continue to stir-fry over high heat for 2 minutes. Add the meat and gravy from the frying-pan. Turn, toss and stir for 1 minute. Sprinkle the contents with M.S.G. and the remaining sherry. Continue to stir-fry gently for ½ minute. Pour the contents into a serving bowl, and serve, capping the dish with the omelette.

Sweet and Sour Pork

This dish should require no introduction, as it must be one of the two or three most popular Chinese dishes served in the West today. Probably more of it is consumed in the Chinese restaurants of Europe and the Americas than ever was in Canton, the city of its origin!

Perhaps westerners are more sweet-toothed than the Chinese; they seem to take to this dish with such enthusiasm. A well-prepared sauce should be bright, translucent, and reddish in colour. The redness comes either from the tomato purée or the minute amount of Chinese red food colouring used. The sauce should be somewhat syrupy in consistency, but not sticky, and it should be mildly sharp and quite refreshing (from the fruit juice used or the vegetables fried in the oil), but the meaty content of the dish should predominate.

Lean pork should be used, and often not cut in cubes, but in oblong pieces approximately 1 in. × ½ in. × ¼ in. Belly pork can be used so long as the skin and fatty parts are removed. Then the pieces are lightly battered and fried over high heat until they begin to get crisp; they are turned in the sauce for ½–1 minute, and served immediately; or sometimes the sauce is simply poured over the hot pieces of pork on the serving dish, so that when they are eaten there is a distinct sensation that the meat is, at least, a few degrees hotter than the warm sauce.

There are many versions of this dish, as with the majority of Chinese dishes. The chief regional variations come from Canton where they tend to introduce fruit juices of all kinds into the sauce, such as orange juice, apple juice, and lichee juice. (I once came across a famous chef who liked to add blackcurrant jam!) In Szechuan, West China, a drop of chilli oil is often added to the various fruity constituents, or one or two pieces of dried chilli are fried in the oil with the vegetables. In the North, in Peking or Tientsin, the inclination is towards a plainer sauce, relying for its effect on the principal ingredients, which are sugar, vinegar, and cornflour, with a drop of wine and soya sauce. I like to add chopped orange or lemon peel to the frying-pan just before pouring in the sauce.

When westerners first experiment with this dish in their own kitchens, their first reaction is usually that an almost inconceivable amount of sugar is added to the savoury meat dish. In my experience the following proportions seem to strike the right balance; 2½ units of sugar, 2 units vinegar,

1½ units cornflour, 1½ units soya sauce, 1½ units tomato
purée, 1 unit sherry, 1 unit orange juice, 4 units water (where
tablespoons are the unit this gives sufficient sauce for 1½–2
lb. of pork).

When the dish is badly prepared, the sauce is not bright,
red, and translucent, but heavy, impure, dark, and clogged.
In this case the cook probably did not filter the oil, used stale
oil, or did not bother to add some red food colouring or
tomato purée. Another fault may be that the meat is too
fatty, or that the actual pieces of meat are tiny, but encased
in very thick batter, which absorbs too much oil in the frying
process. The worst is when this combination of meat and
sauce is served lukewarm, with the meat cooler than the
sauce (this can easily happen if the pre-fried pork is allowed
to cool and then turned in the sauce for too short a time
before serving). You may also find that large quantities of
vegetables are padding out the dish to make up for too little
meat.

SWEET AND SOUR PORK   (for 4–8 people with other dishes)

1½ lb. pork (more lean than fat)
½ teaspoon salt
1 tablespoon soya sauce
½ egg
1 tablespoon cornflour
4 tablespoons water
1 medium onion
1 green or red sweet pepper

for sauce

2½ tablespoons sugar
2 tablespoons vinegar
1½ tablespoons cornflour
1½ tablespoons soya sauce
1 tablespoon sherry (or red wine)
1½ tablespoons tomato purée

4 tablespoons water
1 tablespoon orange juice

vegetable oil for deep-frying

Cut pork into ¾ in. cubes. Rub with salt, add soya sauce and marinate for 1 hour. Blend egg, cornflour and water into a batter; lightly batter the pieces of pork.

Chop onion finely, and slice pepper into strips. Blend the ingredients for the sauce into a smooth mixture in a bowl (it should be stirred and beaten again for 10 seconds just before cooking).

Deep-fry the battered pork in hot oil for 3–3½ minutes. Drain and put aside, and keep very hot (in the oven).

Heat 2 tablespoons oil in a large frying-pan. Fry the chopped onion in it for 1 minute over high heat. Add pepper and stir-fry for another minute. Lower heat and pour in the sauce mixture. Stir until sauce thickens. Add the pork, and turn the pieces gently in the sauce (still over moderate heat) for ½ minute and serve immediately.

Barbecued Spare Ribs

Spare ribs are a good ice-breaker to start a Chinese dinner in the West, because one has to use one's fingers, which immediately establishes the informality and lack of restraint which is essential to the Chinese attitude to food. Chewed bones can even be left on the table (although a side plate is usually provided) and soup can be poured into the rice bowls.

Moreover the expression 'the nearer the bone the sweeter the meat' comes into its own with spare ribs, since all the meat comes immediately off the bone.

Well-prepared ribs are meaty and trimmed of any tough gristle, and the meat comes quite easily off the bones. The meat is very spicy. One of the commonest mistakes in cooking spare ribs is to roast the ribs too long, so that the meat becomes too dry and flaky or tough, instead of being tasty and succulent. In my experience it is best to braise or stew the ribs for a good while before grilling or roasting them. Roasting is the simplest. The other common mistake is not to cook the meat for long enough, so that the meat is too tough to tear off the bones.

SPARE RIBS   (for 4–6 people with other dishes)

3 lb. spare ribs
1 teaspoon salt
2 cloves crushed garlic
2 slices root ginger (finely chopped)
4 tablespoons chopped onion
3 teaspoons sugar
4 tablespoons soya sauce
3 tablespoons dry sherry
⅙ teaspoon five-spice powder (optional)
freshly ground pepper
4 tablespoons vegetable oil
1 cup of good broth

Cut the spare ribs into individual ribs and rub with salt. Heat oil in a frying-pan. Add onion, garlic and ginger. Stir-fry for 1 minute over high heat. Add the ribs. Continue to stir-fry for 5 minutes. Add soya sauce, pepper, five-spice, sherry and sugar. Continue to stir-fry over moderate heat for 2 minutes. Add broth. Stir and turn the ribs in the liquid, until all parts of the ribs are equally browned by the sauce. Lower the heat to a slow simmer. Cover the pan with a lid and allow the contents to cook very gently for 20 minutes. Open the lid, stir and turn the ribs over, then cover and allow to cook for a further ten minutes.

Spread the ribs on to a roasting pan, or flat open casserole. Put the pan or casserole into an oven pre-heated to 375°F, gas 5, to roast and dry for 8–10 minutes; serve. (Heat a little longer in the oven if they are still too wet.)

Fried Rice

Fried rice has many variations, as it merely involves frying cooked rice with any number of ingredients from two to six. The basic ingredients are onion, egg and ham (or bacon). Other popular additions which are fried together with the basic ingredients are chicken, prawns (shrimps), pork, beef, peas, mushrooms (button), chopped cucumbers, and bamboo-shoots.

In cooking fried rice aim at aroma, taste, and contrast in texture and colour. It is usually best to fry the different ingredients in groups, and then combine them at the end, as is common practice in Chinese cooking. One of the things to avoid is frying the rice into a soggy mess.

Fried rice is really a Chinese snack, but being self-contained, it is a good dish to order if you do not intend to have a large selection of dishes. Because it is meant to be a dry dish it is best eaten with a savoury soup (recipes for a few soups follow this recipe). Since it is basically a snack, it is never served at a Chinese banquet – any more than you would serve scrambled egg on toast at a mayoral banquet!

FRIED RICE   (for 3–4 people)

4 eggs
1 teaspoon salt
4 oz. pork (diced into pea-sized pieces)
1½ tablespoons soya sauce
½ teaspoon sugar
6 tablespoons vegetable oil
2 medium onions (chopped)
4 tablespoons green peas
4 tablespoons button mushrooms
2 oz. ham (diced)
½ lb. boiled rice

Beat eggs with half the salt for 10 seconds. Marinate diced pork in soya sauce and sugar. Heat 2 tablespoons oil in a very large frying-pan. Add chopped onion and stir-fry gently for 1 minute. Add peas and mushrooms and ham and continue to fry for ½ minute, and push them to one side of the pan. Add 2 tablespoons oil to the centre of the pan; when hot pour in the beaten egg. When it sets, scramble and push to the opposite side of the pan from the other ingredients. Take the pan off the fire. Heat the remaining oil in the centre of another pan; when very hot pour in the marinated pork. Stir-fry quickly for 3 minutes. Add the cooked rice and scramble and mix with the pork thoroughly for 1 minute.

Pour the rice and pork into the centre of the large frying-pan, sprinkle with remaining salt and scramble and mix with the egg and other ingredients over high heat for 1 minute. Serve on a warmed dish to be eaten immediately (otherwise it will become greasy).

Soups

BASIC BROTH FOR SOUPS OR HIGH BROTH

Boil a chicken carcass and 2 lb. spare ribs in 3½ pints water for 5 minutes. Skim off the scum. Add 1 teaspoon salt, 2 slices root ginger and leave to simmer very gently for 1½ hours. Remove carcass and ribs and check the seasoning (add ½ chicken stock cube). The broth is now ready and will be strong enough to give that unique flavour which is characteristic of all good Chinese soups.

EGG FLOWER SOUP   (for 4–6 people)

1 egg
1½–2 pints high broth (see above)
1½ tablespoons chopped chives (or the green stalk of spring onion)
½ teaspoon sesame oil

This is one of the simplest of the Chinese soups and is sometimes also known as Soup of the Gods.

Beat the egg for 10 seconds. Bring the broth to the boil and lower heat to a simmer. Trail the egg into the soup in the thinnest possible stream along the prongs of a fork. Do not stir the soup until the egg has coagulated (in 15 seconds). Put a drop of sesame oil and a pinch of chopped chives at the bottom of each bowl. Pour the soup into the bowls and serve. The soup should be highly aromatic and very tasty in spite of its simplicity, and is an excellent accompaniment to fried rice throughout a meal.

SLICED MEAT AND CUCUMBER SOUP (for 4–6 people)

4 in. segment of cucumber (with the skin)
2 oz. lean and fat pork
1½ teaspoons cornflour
½ teaspoon salt
dash of pepper
1½–2 pints high broth (see page 90)
1 chicken stock cube

Slice cucumber along the skin into double matchstick size strips.

Slice pork into razor thin slices ¾ in. × ¼ in. Rub with salt and sprinkle with cornflour, working them into the pork.

Bring the broth to the boil in a saucepan, add the pork and simmer for 5 minutes. Add the cucumber and chicken stock cube, sprinkle with pepper, and leave to simmer for a further 3 minutes and serve. This is a savoury but fresh-tasting soup.

CRAB AND SWEET CORN SOUP

1½ pints high broth (see page 90)
1 chicken stock cube
2 slices root ginger
1 can good quality crab (or 4–5 ozs. crab meat)
1 large can sweet corn
2 tablespoons dry sherry
pepper to taste

1½ tablespoons cornflour (blended in 4 tablespoons water)
1½ tablespoons chopped ham
1 tablespoon chopped chives

Add ginger and stock cube to the broth. Heat until it boils.
Pour in the sweet corn and crab meat. Stir until all lumpy
pieces have broken up. When the soup comes to the boil
again, add pepper and sherry, and cornflour to thicken. Pour
soup into individual serving bowls, sprinkle with chopped
chives and chopped ham and serve.

Chow Mein

Chow Mein means Fried Noodles – from *chow* to fry and
mein noodles. Chinese noodles are prepared in a number of
different forms, notably tossed noodles (Pan Mein), assembled
noodles (Hui Mein), cooked (Wo Mein) in thick sauce (Lu
Mein), in soup (Tang Mein) and, finally, fried, Chow Mein.

If Marco Polo had been a professional cookery writer he
might have introduced many forms of noodles to Italy five or
six hundred years ago, to be adapted locally. As it was,
Italians have missed out on the shredded raw vegetables –
such as cucumber, radish, carrots, leeks and spring onion –
which normally accompany noodles in China, and which
add dimension to pastas. Chinese noodle dishes are also dis-
tinguished by aromatic ingredients such as vinegar and
sesame oil, which are essential to their character and quality.

After Marco Polo, it took another five hundred years for
the Chinese labourers coming to the West to introduce
Chow Mein. Chow Mein probably caught on because of the
convenience and speed with which it could be prepared.

CHOW MEIN   (for 4 people)

1 lb. noodles (or spaghetti)
1½ lb. lean pork (or beef)

3 Chinese dried mushrooms
5 tablespoons vegetable oil
1 clove garlic (crushed)
3 spring onions (1 in. segments)
3 oz. shredded cabbage (or celery)
1 oz. bamboo-shoots
½ teaspoon salt
2½ tablespoons soya sauce
1 teaspoon sugar
2 tablespoons dry sherry
2 tablespoons shelled shrimps

Boil the noodles (or spaghetti) until soft. Drain and rinse under cold running water to prevent stickiness.

Slice meat into matchstick strips. Soak dried mushrooms in warm water for ½ hour and slice them into strips or shreds.

Heat 1 tablespoon oil in a large frying-pan. Add garlic, onion, cabbage, bamboo-shoots, and half the salt and stir-fry for 2 minutes over high heat. Remove and put aside.

Add 2 tablespoons oil into the same pan. When very hot add the meat and mushrooms and stir-fry over high heat for 3 minutes (1 minute for beef). Add the soya sauce and sugar and half the sherry and stir-fry for a further minute. Remove with a slotted spoon and put aside.

Add the remaining oil to the pan and then the noodles and the shrimps to be stir-fried with the gravy and oil left in the pan from previous fryings. When the noodles are heated through and browned all over with gravy and oil (about 1½ minutes) add remaining salt, half the meat and half the cooked vegetables which had been put aside. After a further minute of slow stir-frying, dish out on to a warmed serving dish.

Now return the remainder of the vegetables and meat to the same pan together with the rest of the sherry. After a few sizzling turns over high heat (about 15 seconds), spoon the mixed contents of the pan as garnish over the noodles and serve. To connoisseurs of Chow Mein the gravy-flavoured noodles are even more delicious than the meat.

Cha Shao Roast Pork

Although there is an infinite number of pure pork dishes, and as many dishes where pork and other foods are cooked in combination, the most commonly served in Chinese restaurants abroad is Cha Shao Roast Pork, roughly translated as marinated strips of roast pork. It is a regional Cantonese dish particularly convenient since it is excellent hot or cold. In western kitchens using thermostatically controlled ovens, it is even easier to prepare than in China itself.

CHA SHAO ROAST PORK   (for 4–6 people with other dishes)

2 lb. pork fillet
2 tablespoons peanut oil
2 tablespoons honey

for marinade

4 tablespoons soya sauce
1 tablespoon sugar
2 tablespoons sherry
¼ teaspoon pepper
¼ teaspoon powdered cinnamon
1 clove garlic (crushed)
½ teaspoon salt
½ teaspoon M.S.G.
¼ teaspoon mixed herbs

Slice pork along grain into strips 5–6 ins. long, 1½ ins. wide and 1 in. thick.

Mix all the ingredients for the marinade well, add it to the pork in a deep dish and let stand for 2 hours, turning the pork every 15 minutes.

Pre-heat the oven to 425°F, gas 7. Drain the pork (keeping marinade for further use), and place the strips across the rack over a roasting-pan containing some water to catch the drips, to roast for 12 minutes. Brush the pork strips with marinade and peanut oil (or sesame oil). Return the pork to the oven to cook at 350°F, gas 4, for 10 minutes. Brush pork with honey and roast for a further 5 minutes.

When ready to serve, the pork strips should be sliced against grain into ¼ in. slices, and eaten with mustard or soya-chilli dips (see p. 239).

Chicken and Mushrooms

Chicken and Mushrooms in Chinese restaurants usually means sliced chicken breast quick-fried with mushrooms. This is a wet-fried dish where there is a certain amount of sauce, and is very quickly and easily prepared. Preferably use Chinese dried mushrooms, which are much more tasty and meaty than fresh mushrooms, but be sure to soak and wash them well, so that they don't discolour the chicken when fried together. (In the absence of Chinese mushrooms, fresh mushrooms can be used.)

CHICKEN AND MUSHROOMS (for 4–6 people with other dishes)

6 large Chinese dried mushrooms (or ¼ lb. fresh mushrooms)
6 oz. chicken breast
1 tablespoon finely chopped onion
1 slice root ginger (chopped)
½ teaspoon salt
1 dessertspoon light soya sauce
3 tablespoons chicken broth
1 tablespoon dry sherry
3 teaspoons cornflour
½ chicken stock cube (crushed)
3 tablespoons vegetable oil

Soak mushrooms in 1 cup of boiling water for 40 minutes

turning them over half-way through. Retain three table-spoons mushroom water. Slice each mushroom into four. Slice chicken meat into thin 1 in. × ½ in. slices, rub with salt and half the cornflour and put aside for 20 minutes.

Heat 2 tablespoons oil in a frying-pan. When hot, add ginger and onion and stir-fry for 15 seconds; add pieces of chicken and stir-fry for 45 seconds. Remove chicken, etc., and keep warm.

Add the rest of the oil to the frying-pan, and fry the mush-rooms for 1½ minutes. Return the chicken to the pan, add all the other ingredients and stir-fry together for half a minute. Finally add remaining cornflour mixed in 3 tablespoons chicken broth and continue to stir-fry for another ½ minute over high heat. Dish out onto a warmed dish and serve immediately.

Chicken and Almonds

Chicken and Almonds is very similar to the previous recipe, except it is somewhat drier, and the almonds have to be crisped (if they are not already) by roasting or dry-frying (usually the latter). This dish is popular because of the combination of the familiar with the exotic.

CHICKEN AND ALMONDS (for 4–6 people with other dishes).

8 oz. chicken breast
1 teaspoon salt
1 dessertspoon cornflour
2 oz. bamboo-shoots
4 oz. almonds
3 tablespoons vegetable oil
1 tablespoon chopped onion
1 slice root ginger (chopped)
1 tablespoon dry sherry
2 tablespoons high broth (see page 90)
½ chicken stock cube (crushed)
dash of pepper

Cut chicken into 1½ in. × ½ in. slices, rub salt and half cornflour evenly into the chicken. Cut bamboo-shoots similarly. Blanch almonds, and heat carefully in 1 tablespoon oil in a small frying-pan over low heat until crisp. Be careful not to let them get too brown. Put aside and keep hot.

Heat the remaining oil in a large frying-pan. When hot, add onion and ginger and stir-fry for ½ minute. Spread the sliced chicken and bamboo-shoots well out in the pan and continue to stir-fry for 1 minute. Add remaining cornflour mixed in two tablespoons broth and one tablespoon sherry and stir-fry together for ½ minute with the chicken and bamboo-shoots, adding stock cube and pepper. Finally add almonds, turn once or twice, and serve immediately.

These two chicken dishes are typical of the way in which chicken is stir-fried with various different vegetables; cucumber, pimento, bamboo-shoots, or almost any other vegetable can be used in the same manner.

Quick-fried Beef with Ribbons of Onion

Although beef is not as common in China as pork (due to its scarcity), it is not unpopular. In Chinese restaurants abroad there are always one or two beef dishes. This dish is a particular favourite of westerners because of its similarity to beef steak, except that it is more tender!

QUICK-FRIED BEEF WITH RIBBONS OF ONION (for 4–6 people with other dishes)

3 medium onions
1 lb. beef steak (fillet or rump)
½ teaspoon salt
2 teaspoons sugar
dash of pepper
4 teaspoons cornflour
2 tablespoons soya sauce
2 tablespoons dry sherry
½ chicken stock cube (crushed)

T–D

4 tablespoons vegetable oil
2 slices root ginger (shredded)

Cut onion into very thin slices. Cut beef into matchstick
strips. Sprinkle salt, sugar, pepper, and half the cornflour
over the beef and work them in. Add soya sauce and half the
sherry and marinate for 15 minutes. Mix remaining
cornflour and stock cube in 3 tablespoons water and remaining
sherry and put aside. Heat half the oil in a frying-pan. When
hot add the onions and ginger, and stir-fry over high heat for
3 minutes; remove and put aside.

Add remaining oil to the pan. When hot pour in the marinated beef and marinade, and spread it well out on the pan.
Stir-fry for 1½ minutes. Return the onions, toss and stir-fry
together for ½ minute. Add the cornflour mixture, stir-fry for
another 15 seconds and serve immediately on a warmed serving dish.

Crab (or Prawn) Fu-Yung

There always seem to be many more seafood than fish dishes
in Chinese restaurants abroad. This is partly because the
Chinese tend to cook fish whole which makes it difficult to
divide them into standard-sized portions. Fish cooked in slices
must be absolutely fresh, as otherwise it will break into un-
sightly pieces when it is stir-fried; so the cooking of such fish
dishes is a very delicate operation and in the rush and tumble
of an average restaurant kitchen inconvenient to prepare. As
for seafoods – especially prawns and shrimps – they can be
divided into any size portion you please. Besides, even a small
amount adds a great deal of flavour to a dish.

CRAB FU-YUNG   (for 4–6 people with other dishes)

5 eggs
1 teaspoon salt

dash of pepper
2 medium tomatoes
1 medium onion (chopped)
1 clove garlic (crushed)
2 slices root ginger (shredded)
4 tablespoons vegetable oil
6 oz. crab meat
1½ tablespoons dry sherry

Add half the salt and the pepper to the eggs and beat for 10 seconds. Blanch and skin the tomatoes and cut each into six.

Heat 2 tablespoons oil in a frying-pan. Add the onion and stir-fry for 1 minute. Add the garlic and ginger and stir-fry for ½ minute. Finally add the crab meat and remaining salt and stir-fry together for 1 minute and then take off the heat.

Heat the remaining oil in another pan and spread it out evenly. Add the tomatoes and pour in the eggs. Shake and tilt the pan so that the egg spreads out evenly and does not stick. As soon as three quarters of the egg coagulates scramble it lightly together. Pour in the crab meat etc., and scramble lightly together. Pour in the sherry. Toss and scramble a little more, and then turn out on a warmed dish and serve.

Notice that in Chinese cooking western-type omelettes are not common. Eggs are usually lightly scrambled with other foods, although in restaurants abroad they are often prepared like omelettes to conform to the customers' preferences. The combination of crab (or prawns) with egg, and a dash of sherry is typically Chinese.

Deep-fried Giant Prawns

Giant prawns abound along the coastline of North China. In England they are often called Pacific prawns and often measure 3–4 ins. in length. A way of preparing them is deep-frying them in the form of Phoenix Tail Prawns, which the British particularly like and which are convenient to handle.

DEEP-FRIED PHOENIX TAIL PRAWNS

1 lb. giant Pacific prawns
1 slice root ginger (finely chopped)
3 tablespoons plain flour
2 teaspoons self-raising flour
1 egg
6 tablespoons water
½ teaspoon salt

Clean prawns thoroughly and scrape away any dark gritty material. Shell them but leave the tail firmly on and un-shelled (to use as handle).

Beat egg for 15 seconds. Fold in salt, flour, ginger and water. Beat for 30 seconds into a light batter.

Dip each of the prawns into the batter holding on to its tail, and then lower it into a pan of boiling oil; fry 3 or 4 prawns at a time in this way for 2 minutes. Remove them with a perforated spoon and drain. Repeat until a dozen prawns have been fried. If a proper deep-fryer is used, a dozen prawns can be fried at the same time in a wire-basket. Drain them thoroughly on absorbent paper. Arrange them neatly in a pattern on a well-heated plate and serve. It is important that they are eaten with the correct table dips, namely, salt and pepper mix, or soya-tomato dip (with a slight touch of chilli oil added if desired) (see p. 239).

Shrimps and Peas

Stir-frying shrimps with green peas is one of the simplest operations imaginable. To start with, the basic ingredients

are the right size and shape, and require no further chopping
or cutting; besides they are of bright contrasting colours and
take no more than a minute to cook. In practice, however,
most Chinese add chopped Chinese dried mushrooms out of
sheer habit of combining foods, and perhaps a small amount
of abalone (also called awabi) which adds extra tastiness, and
an equally small quantity of diced chicken meat which provides a further contrast in colour and texture.

QUICK-FRIED SHRIMPS WITH PEAS AND ABALONE

(for 4–6 people with other dishes)

2–3 oz. chicken breast
1–2 oz. abalone
1½ teaspoons cornflour
1 teaspoon salt
2–3 black Chinese mushrooms
4 tablespoons vegetable oil
1 tablespoon chopped onion
1 clove crushed garlic
1 slice root ginger (chopped)
½ lb. shelled shrimps
½ lb. green peas
1½ teaspoons sugar
dash of pepper
2 tablespoons sherry
4 tablespoons chicken broth
2 teaspoons cornflour (blended in 2½ tablespoons water)

Dice chicken and abalone into cubes about the size of the
peas. Sprinkle the cornflour and ¼ teaspoon of salt over the
chicken and rub in. Soak mushrooms in a cupful of warm
water for 20 minutes and chop into pieces the size of peas.

Heat 2 tablespoons oil in a frying-pan. When hot, add
onion, garlic and ginger and stir-fry for 1 minute. Add the
shrimps and abalone and stir-fry for 1 minute; remove and
put aside.

Add the remaining oil to the pan, and stir-fry the chicken and mushrooms over moderate heat for ½ minute. Now add the peas and turn up the heat to the maximum, and continue to fry, stirring gently, for 1½ minutes. Return the shrimps and abalone to the pan and mix with the other ingredients. Sprinkle with sugar, a dash of pepper and remaining salt, pour in the sherry, chicken broth and cornflour mixture. Stir-fry together for ½ minute and serve immediately in a warmed plain-coloured serving dish.

Braised Duck with Pineapple (or Orange)

There are usually one or two duck dishes on a Chinese res-taurant menu, usually Duck with Pineapple or Duck with Orange (perhaps in deference to westerners' taste for the well-known French dish). Both are prepared in much the same way – the duck braised with soya sauce and the fruit added only in the final hot assembly. One starts by preparing the soya-braised duck.

SOYA-BRAISED DUCK (in one dish for 6–8 people, or in 2 dishes with pineapple and orange for 8–12 people together with other dishes)

1 duck (3–4 lb.)
3 slices root ginger (chopped)
2 medium onions (chopped)
1 teaspoon salt
1 teaspoon sugar (malt)
6 tablespoons soya sauce
¼ pint water
2 spring onions (cut in segments)
6 tablespoons vegetable oil

Clean duck and wipe it dry. Rub the inside of the duck with a mixture of salt, chopped ginger and onion. Paint the outside of the duck with a mixture of malt sugar and soya sauce, rubbing it in. Repeat this operation twice more at 15 minute intervals and collect the marinade.

Brown the duck quickly in an oven pre-heated to 400°F, gas 6, for 15 minutes. Remove the duck from the oven, and turn it in hot oil in a large saucepan for 2–3 minutes. Drain away oil. Add spring onion segments, water, and the remainder of the marinade; bring to the boil and simmer gently for 20 minutes, turn it over and simmer gently for another 20 minutes.

Joint the duck and chop into sixteen pieces. Re-assemble on a serving dish, pour the hot gravy over the duck and serve.

BRAISED DUCK WITH PINEAPPLE (for 5–6 people with other dishes)

½ soya-braised duck (with gravy)
6 slices pineapple
½ cup pineapple juice
3 teaspoons cornflour (mixed in 2 tablespoons water)
2 tablespoons sherry

Joint and chop the braised duck as in previous recipe and arrange on serving dish. Mix the pineapple juice with cornflour mixture. Cut each slice of pineapple into four.

Drain some of the fat from the duck gravy, and heat the gravy in a small saucepan. Pour in the pineapple juice, sherry and cornflour mixture. Stir over gentle heat until the mixture thickens. Garnish the duck with the pineapple pieces, pour the pineapple gravy over the duck and serve.

BRAISED DUCK WITH ORANGE

is prepared in a similar manner, substituting orange for pineapple, using 8 slices of orange and half a cup of strained fresh orange juice to which 2 teaspoons sugar have been added for the sauce.

Fried Mixed Vegetables

Although fried mixed vegetables should not be ordered in a
Chinese restaurant for reasons already mentioned, it is a good
dish to cook at home being a dish for all seasons – a kind of
Chinese hot salad.

FRIED MIXED VEGETABLES (for 4–8 people with other
dishes)

4 oz. carrot
4 oz. cauliflower
5 oz. spring greens
½ cup good chicken broth
½ chicken stock cube (crumbled)
5 tablespoons vegetable oil
1 slice root ginger
1 clove garlic (crushed)
1½ teaspoons salt
dash of pepper
¼ teaspoon chilli powder
1 teaspoon sugar
2 teaspoons soya sauce
2 tablespoons chicken fat
5 oz. bean sprouts
2 teaspoons vinegar
1 teaspoon sesame oil

Slice carrot into thin slices, breaking cauliflower into 1 in.
size flowerets, cut greens into 1–1½ in. pieces (discard outer
leaves). Mix stock cube with chicken broth.

Heat 2 tablespoons oil in the centre of a large frying-pan
(with lid). When hot stir-fry ginger and half the garlic in it
for 15 seconds. Add carrot and stir-fry for 2 minutes. Sprinkle
with ½ teaspoon salt and pepper, mix and turn a few times
and push to one side of the pan.

Add 1½ tablespoons oil and the rest of the garlic to the
centre of the pan and stir-fry the cauliflower in it for 2

minutes. Sprinkle with ½ teaspoon salt and the chilli powder, and push to the opposite side to the carrots, etc.

Put 1½ tablespoons oil in the centre of the pan, and stir-fry the greens in it for 1½ minutes. Sprinkle with sugar and soya sauce, mix and turn and pour in three tablespoons chicken broth. Pour two tablespoons of broth over the carrot and two tablespoons over the cauliflower. Place a lid over the pan, and leave the contents to simmer gently for 3 minutes.

Meanwhile, heat chicken fat in a separate frying-pan or saucepan. Stir-fry the bean sprouts over high heat for 1 minute. Add the rest of the salt, chicken broth, vinegar and a couple of drops of sesame oil and continue to stir-fry for 1 minute.

By this time the vegetables in the large frying-pan should be nearly ready. Open the lid and pour a spoonful or two of chicken broth and a drop of sesame oil over each group of vegetables, and stir gently. Ladle out the carrots first, placing them at the centre of a large warmed dish. Then arrange the cauliflower in a ring around the carrots, and the spring greens around the cauliflower. Finally, place the bean sprouts around the greens in the outer ring. This arrangement of vegetables in concentric rings not only presents a contrast in colour, but also a difference in flavour reflecting both the variety of materials and also the difference in seasonings.

Crispy Meat Balls

In China, large meat balls are a banquet dish called Lion's Heads. They are served with salt and pepper mix or soya–tomato dips (with a touch of chilli oil to add pungency). They are usually presented on a bed of vegetables such as dried lily buds or spinach, with gravy.

The meat balls served in Chinese restaurants are dry and crisp and perhaps more appetizing, except when Lion's Heads are perfectly made. Chinese meat balls differ from the average western variety in that chopped water chestnuts are added for crunchiness and pork fat for succulence.

CRISPY MEAT BALLS   (for 6 people with other dishes)

1½ lb. lean minced pork
2 oz. pork fat (coarsely chopped)
3 oz. water chestnuts (coarsely chopped)
1 slice root ginger (finely chopped)
1 medium onion (finely chopped)
2 teaspoons sugar
1 teaspoon salt
2 tablespoons soya sauce
3 tablespoons cornflour
1 egg
vegetable oil for deep-frying

Mix all the above ingredients (except the oil) together to a smooth consistency; form 12 balls.

Heat the oil in a deep-fryer until hot. Lower the meat balls into the oil in a wire basket to fry for 2½ minutes. Lift the basket and drain meat balls for 3 minutes. Re-immerse the meat balls to fry for a further 2 minutes; they will be well cooked and crisp and ready to serve.

Spring Rolls (or Pancake Rolls)

Spring rolls are simply thin dough sheets stuffed with savoury fillings and then deep-fried. The dough is made from plain flour, egg and water, rolled paper thin, and cut into pieces 8 ins. × 8 ins. The pancakes can also be made in the usual manner pancakes are made in the West – with thin batter. The fillings are cooked before they are wrapped in the dough so that the frying need not be prolonged. When the stuffing has been rolled up, and the ends folded in, the last edge is secured by moistening it with beaten egg.

SPRING ROLLS (makes 10 rolls)

for dough

4 cups flour
2 cups water
1 egg

for filling

3 tablespoons lard
½ lb. pork (shredded)
½ lb. bean sprouts
4 spring onions (chopped into 1 in. segments)
1 teaspoon salt
1½ tablespoons soya sauce
pepper
1½ teaspoons sugar
2 tablespoons mushrooms (chopped)
2 tablespoons shrimps (peeled)

vegetable oil for deep-frying

Knead the flour, water and half the egg into a smooth dough and roll into a very thin sheet. Cut sheet into 10 square pieces (approx. 8 ins. × 8 ins.).

Heat the lard in a frying-pan. When hot, add the pork and salt and stir-fry for 2 minutes. Add all the other ingredients and stir-fry together for another 2 minutes; put aside and allow to cool.

Divide the fried stuffings into 10 portions and place each portion on a piece of dough (just below the centre). Roll up from the bottom two thirds of the way and fold in the two ends. Continue to roll up, moisten the top edge with beaten egg and press down.

Deep-fry five rolls at a time in hot oil for 3½ minutes and drain on absorbent paper. Keep hot while the second batch of rolls is being fried.

Quick-fried Sliced Pork with Broccoli

This recipe uses a well known technique: as pork is the most popular meat in China, and often one of the cheapest in the West, and quick stir-frying one of the most economical and efficient forms of cooking, we may as well go through the method once more.

QUICK-FRIED SLICED PORK WITH BROCCOLI

1 lb. lean pork
1 teaspoon salt
3 teaspoons cornflour
1 slice root ginger (chopped finely)
¾ lb. broccoli
4 tablespoons vegetable oil
1 medium onion (chopped)
4 tablespoons chicken broth
2 teaspoons sugar
1¾ tablespoons soya sauce
2 tablespoons sherry
½ chicken stock cube (crushed)
pepper to taste

Cut pork into very thin slices 1 in. × ½ in. Rub salt, cornflour and ginger thoroughly into the meat. When a small amount of cornflour is rubbed into pork (or chicken) before it is simmered or fried it becomes very smooth. Cut broccoli into approximately 1 in. pieces.

Heat two tablespoons oil in a frying-pan. When hot add pork and onion and stir-fry gently over high heat for 3 minutes. Take out and keep hot.

Add the rest of the oil to the pan and tilt to spread the oil around. Put in the broccoli and stir-fry gently over medium heat for 3 minutes. Sprinkle with chicken broth and sugar and continue to stir-fry for ½ minute; cover pan with a lid and leave to cook for 2 minutes. Add the pork and onion to the broccoli. Sprinkle the contents of the pan with soya sauce, sherry, stock cube and pepper, continue to stir-fry for 1 minute and serve.

Cooking Utensils

The only utensils required to cook all the preceding twenty-one dishes have been an oven, a frying-pan, and one or two saucepans, which should be available in any kitchen. A deep-fryer is useful for cooking spring rolls and giant prawns etc., but in its absence (as so often in China) a frying-pan with ¼–½ pint of oil is quite a satisfactory substitute, with a perforated spoon to turn and ladle out the food. However, it is useful for Chinese cooking to have a lid for the frying-pan, since a little broth or water is often added after quick-frying, and the contents allowed to simmer under cover for 2–3 minutes, before the seasoning is finally adjusted and the dish given a further quick stir-fry.

In the next section of the book we shall be attempting more ambitious and elaborate dishes and we shall need a steamer (preferably an oblong-shaped one for cooking fish), some heavy saucepans and casseroles for long simmering. But do always bear in mind that the elaborate dishes are not necessarily the best; the simplest to prepare are often the most delicious.

Menus using Basic Dishes

So far we have only covered the preparation of twenty-one dishes, but the possible combinations into menus are numerous. In general menus in China take into account the difference in the types of foods, the difference in methods of cooking and textures, and the relation between meat, fish, and vegetable dishes, so that colours, and even food values, are contrasted and balanced.

The following are a few five-dish menus for three or four people:

(1) Egg-flower Soup
     Fried Rice
     Spring Rolls
     Shrimps and Peas
     Quick-fried Beef with
        Onion Ribbons

(2) Sliced Meat and
        Vegetable Soup
     Crispy Meat Balls
     Fried Rice
     Chicken and Mushroom
     Chopsuey

(3) Crab and Sweet-Corn
        Soup
     Chow Mein
     Quick-fried Sliced Pork
        with Broccoli
     Chicken and Almonds
     Sweet and Sour Pork

(4) Spare Ribs
     Fried Rice
     Beef and Onion
     Chao Shao Pork
     Crab Fu-Yung

(5) Spare Ribs
     Fried Rice
     Chopsuey
     Deep-fried Giant Prawns
     Sweet and Sour Pork

(6)   Egg Flower Soup
    Chow Mein
    Quick-fried Beef with
      Onion Ribbons
    Crispy Meat Balls
    Chicken and Almonds

China tea should be served throughout the meal with all the above menus and there should be plenty of boiled rice to accompany the dishes, especially where fried rice is not on the menu.

For people who like alcohol during their meals, most dry white European wines are suitable with Chinese food (but not sweet red wines which are too heavy).

PART THREE

Chinese Cooking in China

The following recipes are grouped according to the four main geographical divisions of China: South, North, East and West-Central; within each division four seasonal menus are provided, each with seven dishes including a soup or sweet. A detailed and practical recipe is given for each dish so that it can be reproduced independently or in the context of the menu.

All the recipes that follow are meant to be part of traditional Chinese communal meals for four to ten people. As already explained, one increases the number of dishes, rather than the individual quantities to feed more people.

Although China is a continental country where the seasons are quite distinct, the spring and autumn are often very short. Before you have even begun to enjoy the first flush of spring the temperature has risen and the long, hot summer begun. September and October are often windless and brilliant with sunshine, yet just as you begin to enjoy the mellow, golden autumn, the north wind blows, the lakes and canals freeze overnight, and you are in the grip of what appears to be an arctic winter. Even in West-Central and Eastern China neither winter nor summer is by any means temperate or short. In grouping dishes for the different seasons, there are a few which can only be served in the summer or winter, but the spring and autumn dishes need not be so strictly classified and can be movable. In making my selection I have been guided by what is most characteristic of the season and area, and also not too complicated and time-consuming to reproduce. Our pilgrimage through the Chinese culinary world starts from Canton, where most westerners enter China from Hongkong.

Seasons in South China

It was in South China that I was born, bred and went to school. The climate is semi-tropical, the summer long, hot, and torrid, and in the afternoons there are often thunderstorms, which help to dispel the heat which, by midday, lies oppressively over the land. Every now and then a muggy monsoon blows fleeting clouds across the sky for several days on end. Otherwise the sun beats down on every object on the earth below until the ground, the stones, and walls all radiate a blistering heat. You might think that in such a climate one would have little appetite. Quite the contrary. I was hungry almost all the time and any sort of food was welcome. The autumn days were brilliant, windless, perfect. Although the school meals were lean and mirrored accurately the generally pitiful subsistence level of life in China, I was able to buy snacks from foodshops or eat a savoury dish or two in small cheap restaurants as soon as school and games were over. The streets were full of food vendors who sold jellied meats and cooked chicken drumsticks with buns, or would cook you a dish of noodles or meat-stuffed wraplings on the spot. Eating became as much an entertainment and recreation as sport itself.

The winters were excessively cold (maybe because there was no heating in the classrooms), but the holidays and the New Year heralded festivities which meant food. The large, steamed and long-simmered dishes, the red-cooked dishes, the earthenware casseroles! They were not only heaven to eat, and available in mountainous quantities, but they managed to warm up every area of the body, until even your toes unfroze.

Spring was the least memorable of the four seasons, perhaps because it was so short, but it was fascinating to watch the bamboo-shoots in the bamboo groves in our garden breaking through the ground and sprouting at the rate of at least an inch a day! Then suddenly the mist and rain were banished by a hot sun, long walks became too enervating, and along the roadside small mounds of peeled water chestnuts were sold, the colour of carved ivory, and eight-to-ten-inch lengths of fat sugar-cane full of sugary juice, which had been scraped with a knife till they were equally spotless and white. After long treks through the hills around the town or competitions against other schools at the city sports fields (where they also conducted occasional executions), we dreamed of chicken and duck, and meat cooked in wine sediment paste, or noodles stewed with leeks and oyster and mushrooms!

Cooking is not just sustenance to a Chinese, it is a part of his cultural heritage.

Spring in Canton

Watercress and Sliced Pork Soup
Sliced Steak in Oyster Sauce

Quick-fried Sweet and Sour Spare Ribs
Crabs in Aromatic Oil
Red-cooked Pork with Dried Squid
Simmered Eel with Cooked Pork and Chestnuts
Crackling Fried Chicken

PORK AND WATERCRESS SOUP

3 oz. lean pork
½ teaspoon salt
2 teaspoons cornflour
2 pints high broth (p. 90)
½ teaspoon M.S.G. (or chicken stock cube)
1 bundle watercress
pepper to taste

Cut pork into thin slices 1 in. × ⅓ in. Rub with salt and dust
with cornflour.

Bring the broth to a gentle boil in a saucepan, add M.S.G.
and lower heat to a simmer. Add the pieces of pork, and allow
them to simmer in the broth for 10 minutes. Clean the watercress thoroughly and add it with the pepper; allow the contents of the pan to simmer for a further three minutes. Serve
in a large bowl or tureen in the middle of the table for the
guests to ladle into their individual bowls.

In China this soup is designated *Ching T'an* which means
clear, pure, and uncomplicated.

SLICED STEAK IN OYSTER SAUCE

1¾ lb. beef steak (rump or fillet)
1 tablespoon cornflour
½ teaspoon salt
pepper
1 tablespoon soya sauce
2 tablespoons oyster sauce
½ teaspoon M.S.G. (or ½ chicken stock cube crushed)

4 tablespoons vegetable oil
1½ tablespoons dry sherry

Cut the steak across the grain into 1½ in. × ½ in. slices.
Rub with salt and pepper to taste and dust thoroughly with
cornflour.

Heat oil in a frying-pan. When very hot add the beef,
spread it evenly over the pan, and stir-fry for 1 minute. Add
the soya sauce and oyster sauce, and sprinkle the beef with
sherry and M.S.G. After a further ½ minute of stir-frying
over high heat turn out on to a warmed dish and serve immediately.

Because of the very short cooking time this highly savoury
dish is full of the original goodness and distinctive flavour of
beef.

QUICK-FRIED SWEET AND SOUR SPARE RIBS

2½ lb. meaty spare ribs
2 tablespoons chopped onion
1 slice root ginger (finely chopped)
1 teaspoon salt
1 clove garlic (crushed)
3 tablespoons vegetable oil

for the sauce

2 tablespoons sugar
2 tablespoons vinegar
1½ tablespoons soya sauce
2 tablespoons tomato purée
2 tablespoons fresh orange juice
1½ tablespoons cornflour (blended with 3 tablespoons water)
½ drop chilli oil

Chop spare ribs into 1 in. pieces. Give each piece a blow
with the side of a heavy chopper. Sprinkle and rub with
salt.

Blend the sauce ingredients in a bowl to a smooth consistency.

Heat oil in a frying-pan. When hot add the spare ribs and stir-fry vigorously over high heat for 5 minutes. Add onion, garlic and ginger. Lower the heat to moderate and continue to stir-fry more gently now, for 5 more minutes. Stir the sauce for 5–6 seconds again and add to the contents of the pan. Continue to stir-fry for ½ minute, then serve on a warmed dish.

In this dish the meatiness of the ribs, and the piquant refreshing qualities of the sauce are equally enjoyable and should complement each other.

QUICK-FRIED CRAB IN AROMATIC OIL

2 fresh crabs
3 tablespoons vegetable oil
1 medium onion (finely chopped)
1 clove garlic (crushed)
2 slices root ginger (finely chopped)
1 teaspoon salt
2 tablespoons finely sliced leek
1 egg (lightly beaten)
5 tablespoons high broth (p. 90)
2 tablespoons dry sherry
3 teaspoons cornflour (blended in 3 tablespoons water)
1 teaspoon M.S.G.
1 teaspoon sesame oil

Clean each crab and chop shell into two and the body into six pieces with each piece attached to a leg or claw. Crack each claw with a blow or two from the side of the chopper.

Heat oil in a frying-pan. When very hot add onion, garlic and ginger and stir-fry for a few seconds. Add the pieces of crab and continue to stir-fry for 3 minutes over a high heat. Sprinkle the crabs with salt and the leek and pour the beaten egg over the crab in a thin stream along the prongs of a fork.

After turning and scrambling once or twice, pour in the broth and sherry. Stir for a further ½ minute. Add the blended cornflour, M.S.G., and sesame oil and after a few more seconds of slow stir-frying, turn out on to a warmed dish and serve.

There is a Chinese saying 'After crab everything else is tasteless.' The crab is sucked and chewed heartily (when it comes to this dish, there is not much fastidiousness in China), and the sauce and egg in the dish are just as delicious as the crab meat itself.

RED-COOKED PORK WITH DRIED SQUID

2 lb. lean pork
2 lb. belly pork
6 oz. dried squid (or 1 teaspoon anchovy and ¼ lb. smoked haddock)
2 oz. lily buds (or golden needles)
1 teaspoon salt
6 tablespoons soya sauce
3 slices root ginger
3 teaspoons sugar
4 tablespoons dry sherry

Cut pork into 1½ in. cubes. (The belly pork should be cut so that each piece has both lean and fat and some skin.) Soak the lily buds in water for 20 minutes and cut them in half inch segments. Cut the squid into 2in. × ½ in. strips.

Heat 1½ pints water in a large saucepan, add the pork and boil for 5 minutes. Pour away two thirds of the water. Add ginger, salt, and soya sauce. Cover the contents and simmer gently for 1 hour, turning the pork over twice.

Add the lily buds, dried squids, and sugar and bury them under the pork; add sherry and adjust the seasonings. Add a little water if the gravy is drying up; simmer for another hour with an asbestos sheet under the pan. Turning the contents over twice, serve in a large bowl or deep dish.

The lily buds have a musty flavour, and the dried squid

taste like smoked fish (kippers or smoked haddock). These two flavours impregnate the pork and the gravy and the result is a rich and savoury dish particularly good with rice.

You may prefer to cook this dish in a casserole in the oven at 350°F, gas 4. Apart from the fact that the temperature is more even in the oven than over a flame, the dish can be brought to the table in the casserole.

SIMMERED EEL WITH ROAST PORK AND CHESTNUTS

2–3 eels weighing 3–3½ lb.
4 oz. Cantonese roast pork (p. 94)
6 oz. Chinese dried mushrooms
4 oz. chestnuts
2 tablespoons vegetable oil
2 oz. leeks (thinly sliced)
2 slices root ginger
1 teaspoon salt
1 tablespoon dried tangerine peel
2 teaspoons brown sugar
2 tablespoons light soya sauce
2 tablespoons dry sherry
½ pint water
pepper to taste
1 tablespoon vinegar
1 teaspoon M.S.G.
1 tablespoon cornflour (blended in 3 tablespoons water)
½ teaspoon sesame oil

Clean eels thoroughly and chop into 2 in. lengths. Slice pork thinly. Soak mushrooms in warm water for half an hour, drain and discard stems. Peel the chestnuts, boil in water for ten minutes; discard water.

Heat oil in a heavy iron pan or casserole. Stir-fry for another ½ minute and take off the heat.

Now spread the leeks, ginger, tangerine peel and mushrooms evenly over the bottom of a casserole. Place the chestnuts over them, and then arrange the pieces of eel on top of the chestnuts. Finally place the pieces of pork on top of the eel. Sprinkle with sugar, soya sauce, sherry, gently pour in the water and cover. Heat the casserole over a fire until the contents are just about to boil, then place it in a pre-heated oven at 350°F, gas 4, for 70 minutes when the contents will be ready to serve.

Pick the pieces of eel out of the casserole with a pair of chopsticks or a perforated spoon and put aside on a warmed plate. Scoop all the other solids out and spread them out on the bottom of a serving bowl. Arrange the pieces of eel on top. Sprinkle the eel with pepper and vinegar. Add M.S.G., cornflour and sesame oil to broth in the casserole. Bring to the boil, pour over the eel and serve.

This is another very rich dish and very good with rice.

CRACKLING FRIED CHICKEN

1 roasting chicken (2½–3 lb.)
4 slices root ginger (finely chopped)
2 teaspoons salt
½ tablespoon malt sugar (or ordinary sugar if unavailable)
1½ tablespoons white vinegar
1½ tablespoons light soya sauce
2 tablespoons water
1½ tablespoons sherry
3 tablespoons cornflour
oil for deep-frying

Mix salt and ginger together and rub the chicken thoroughly inside and out. Leave to marinate for 3 hours in an airy place. Chop the chicken into 16—20 pieces.

To chop a chicken into 16–20 pieces the Chinese way, you will need a very sharp heavy cleaver (or a razor sharp Chinese chopper, which is available from Chinese provision shops, costing 75p–£1.50). You first quarter the chicken in the usual way, and then chop each of the legs into three pieces, and each wing into two pieces, giving 10 pieces. You then chop the body into three across and right through the breast bone, and each of these pieces twice, producing 6 pieces. You can eliminate one or two scraggy end pieces, or chop one or two of the larger pieces into two, to end up with 16–20 pieces. Chopping through the bones is made much easier using a very thick chopping board, as the action requires a very firm base. A Chinese chopping board, which is now available from the larger provision stores is about 12–18 ins. in diameter and 6 ins. thick (a slice of the tree trunk) and costs £1.50–£3 or £4.

Mix sugar, vinegar, soya sauce, water, sherry and cornflour into a paste. Rub the pieces of chicken with half of this paste, and leave them to dry in an airy place for two hours. Rub in the remainder of the paste, and leave to dry for 1 more hour.

Heat oil in a deep-fryer until very hot. Deep-fry the chicken in two lots for 3–3½ minutes each when the pieces should be very crisp.

Serve hot, with salt and pepper mix (p. 240) and Tomato Soya Chilli Dip (see p. 239).

This crisp crackling dish, one of the best regional dishes of its type in China, is a good contrast to other softer and wetter dishes. In China the meat is removed from the bones in the mouth, or using fingers or chopsticks.

Summer in Canton

Pure Vegetable Soup
Steamed Spare Ribs with Plums
Lichee Pork
Cold Sliced Red-cooked Pork
Squid with Crab and Tomato Sauce

Chilled Bean Curd
Steamed Chicken with Chinese Salami Sausage
Marrow Bowl

PURE VEGETABLE SOUP

2½ pints of high broth (see p. 90)
2 oz. carrots
2 oz. turnips
½ bundle watercress
2 oz. spinach
2 oz. marrow
2 oz. cucumber
1 oz. transparent (pea-starch) noodles (soaked in hot water for 5–10 minutes)
2 teaspoons dried shrimps
1 teaspoon salt
pepper to taste
1 teaspoon M.S.G. (or 1 chicken stock cube)

Cut carrot and turnip into small cubes or triangular-shaped pieces. Clean spinach and watercress thoroughly, removing the latter's lower stems. Peel the marrow and cut into 2 in. × 1 in. pieces. Cut the cucumber similarly without peeling the skin. Heat broth in a large saucepan. When it starts to boil add turnip, carrot and dried shrimps and leave to simmer slowly for 15 minutes. Add the marrow, watercress and noodles and simmer for 5 minutes. Add the spinach and cucumber and simmer for a further 5 minutes. Sprinkle with salt, M.S.G. and pepper to taste and serve in a large bowl or tureen.

SPARE RIBS WITH PLUMS

2 lb. meaty spare ribs
1 teaspoon salt
3 tablespoons vegetable oil
1 slice root ginger (chopped)

3 teaspoons salted black beans (soaked for 20 minutes and mashed)
1 lb. plums (peeled, stoned and halved or quartered if large)
3 teaspoons sugar
2 tablespoons light soya sauce
2 tablespoons sherry
1 tablespoon cornflour

Chop ribs into 1½ in. lengths. Give each piece a blow with side of chopper. Rub with salt.

Heat oil in a frying-pan. When hot add ginger and salted beans. Stir-fry for 1½ minutes. Add spare ribs and stir-fry over high heat for five minutes.

Transfer the ribs to a basin. Add plums, sugar, soya sauce, sherry, cornflour and mix gently. Place the basin in a steamer or double boiler and steam vigorously for 30 minutes.

Serve in the original bowl or put spare ribs and plums into a deep dish to serve.

Another way of making this dish is to pack the ribs at the bottom of a basin, and pile the plums and all the ingredients on top (allowing juices to drip through). When steamed for one hour turn the contents out like a pudding and serve.

LICHEE PORK

In this dish, the lichee is like the orange in Duck with Orange; the lichees are used as garnish and the juice in the sauce.

2 lb. lean belly pork
1 teaspoon salt
1 tablespoon soya sauce
1 tablespoon sherry

for the batter

1 lightly beaten egg
2 tablespoons chopped onion
1½ tablespoons cornflour
oil for frying

for the sauce

10 oz. tin lichees (including juice)
2 tablespoons sugar
2 tablespoons vinegar
2 tablespoons sherry
2 tablespoons tomato purée
1 tablespoon cornflour (blended with 3 tablespoons water)

Dice pork into 1 in. cubes, removing the skin. Sprinkle pork with salt, soya sauce and sherry, working them into the pork with fingers. Spread the pieces on a roasting pan and put in the oven at 350°F, gas 4, to dry for 10–12 minutes. When dried, cover with a batter made by blending the cornflour, the lightly beaten egg and the finely chopped onion. Deep-fry the pork in hot oil over moderate heat for 5 minutes. (Or shallow-fry for 6–7 minutes in 6 tablespoons vegetable oil, stirring and turning the pork over continuously.) Meanwhile, mix together all the ingredients for the sauce, keeping aside a few lichees for decoration. Heat gently in saucepan, stirring until sauce thickens. When the pork is ready, place it in a warmed serving dish, pour over the sauce, decorate with a few lichees and arrange the rest of the fruit around the base of the meat.

COLD SLICED RED-COOKED PORK

4 lb. leg of pork
2 pork trotters
6 tablespoons soya sauce
2 tablespoons sugar
2 pieces anise star
1 teaspoon salt
½ teaspoon M.S.G. (or 1 crushed chicken stock cube)
4 tablespoons sherry
1½ tablespoons gelatine powder (dissolved in a little cold water)
1¾ pints water
1 tablespoon chopped chives

Place the pork and trotters in a pan of water. Boil for 5
minutes and pour away the water.

Add sugar, soya sauce, salt, anise star and 1¾ pints water
to the pan. Bring to boil and allow the contents to simmer
very gently for 2½ hours turning the pork over every 30
minutes (put an asbestos sheet under the pan). Then add
sherry, M.S.G. and gelatine to the broth. After 2
minutes remove the pork and trotters to a large basin, into
which the liquid is then poured. Allow to cool for half an
hour, and then chill in a refrigerator for 3 hours. By this time
the gravy will have set into a jelly. Scrape away the fat on top
and slice the meat into thin slices. Place trotters in the middle
and arrange slices of pork around them on a serving dish.
Spoon the jelly over the trotters and sprinkle with chopped
chives.

This is a good dish for the summer months. The golden
meat jelly contrasts attractively with the neatly sliced red-
cooked meat, and is at least as appetizing as the meat itself. It
can be kept in the refrigerator for 4–5 days.

QUICK-FRIED SQUID WITH CRAB AND TOMATO SAUCE

¾ lb. squid
½ teaspoon salt
2 slices root ginger (chopped)
1 tablespoon onion (finely chopped)
3 tablespoons crab (fresh or cooked)
1½ tablespoons tomato purée
2 teaspoons sugar
1 tablespoon light soya sauce
4 tablespoons chicken broth
1 tablespoon sherry
3 tablespoons vegetable oil
3 teaspoons cornflour (blended with 2 tablespoons water)

Clean squid thoroughly, and rub in salt. Cut into 3 in. × 1 in.
strips and make a dozen criss-cross cuts over one side of each

of the pieces (to stop them curling up).

Heat 2 tablespoons oil in a frying-pan. Stir-fry the onion and ginger in it over medium heat for ½ minute. Add the pieces of squid and continue to stir-fry gently for 2 minutes. Remove and put aside. Add the remaining oil to the pan, and stir-fry the crab in it for ½ minute. Add the chicken broth, soya sauce, sugar, sherry and tomato pureé. Stir until the mixture is well blended. Finally add the cornflour. Stir until the sauce thickens. Add the squid and stir-fry gently for 1 minute and serve.

Squid has an interesting chewy texture, well set off by the crab and tomato sauce. The Cantonese use dried squid extensively as a flavouring, rather more often than fresh.

CHILLED BEAN CURD

3–4 cakes bean curd
2 tablespoons soya sauce
2 tablespoons peanut butter
1 tablespoon wine vinegar
3 tablespoons salad oil
1 teaspoon sesame oil
1 teaspoon sugar
1 teaspoon chilli sauce

Simmer the bean curd in water for 10 minutes, then drain. Place the bean curd in the refrigerator to chill for 1½ hours.

Blend the soya sauce, peanut butter, salad oil, vinegar, sesame oil, sugar and chilli sauce to a smooth consistency.

When the bean curd is well chilled, pour the sauce over it and serve.

This is a favourite summer dish, not only in Canton, but also in the other provinces. The rather bland bean curd is enriched and made savoury by the peanut butter, soya sauce, and chilli, all of which combine to form a peculiarly Chinese delicacy, beloved by everyone.

STEAMED CHICKEN WITH CHINESE SALAMI

1 chicken (2–3 lb.)
4 oz. Chinese salami sausage (about 3 pieces)
6 large Chinese dried mushrooms
3 tablespoons onion (chopped)
2 slices root ginger (finely chopped)
½ teaspoon salt
2 teaspoons sugar
1 tablespoon cornflour
1½ tablespoons light soya sauce
2 tablespoons dry sherry
3 tablespoons soya sauce
1 teaspoon sesame oil

Cooking salami with chicken is very much in the southern tradition.

Soak mushrooms in a cupful of warm water for 20 minutes. Discard stems, cut each mushroom in four. Clean chicken and chop through the bone into 16–20 pieces (see pp. 121–2). Cut salami into slices ¼ in. thick. Place them all in a bowl. Mix the cornflour, onion, ginger, sugar, salt, light soya sauce and sherry well, rub into the chicken, and leave to marinate for half an hour.

Arrange layers of chicken, mushrooms and salami in a heatproof serving dish, add any marinade from the bowl and steam the dish vigorously for 40 minutes.

Heat the 3 tablespoons soya sauce and 1 teaspoon sesame oil together in a small saucepan. Pour evenly over the steamed dish and serve.

MARROW BOWL

One end of large marrow, which will fit snugly into a heatproof bowl
2 oz. chicken or duck liver (diced)
2 oz. Cantonese roast pork (see p. 94)
½ teaspoon salt

2 tablespoons vegetable oil
1 teacup chicken broth
4 oz. chicken breast (diced into ¼ in. cubes)
1 slice root ginger (chopped)
2 oz. button mushrooms
2 oz. fresh shrimps
2–3 oz. cucumber (diced)
2 tablespoons sherry
½ teaspoon M.S.G.
3 teaspoons cornflour blended in 2 tablespoons water
1 oz. smoked ham (finely chopped)

Make a marrow bowl by scooping out marrow carefully, leaving a wall ½ in. thick. Place it in a heatproof bowl of about the same size so that it stands upright.

Stir-fry liver, roast pork and salt in oil for 2 minutes. Drain away any excess oil and place the meat at the bottom of the marrow. Heat the centre part of the marrow which was scooped out, together with some outer segments in 1½ teacups of water for 15 minutes to obtain marrow water. Heat chicken broth in a small saucepan. Add chicken, ginger, mushrooms, shrimps, cucumber, sherry and M.S.G.; simmer together for 15 minutes; add the cornflour. When the liquid thickens slightly, pour the mixture over the pork and liver at the bottom of the scooped-out marrow. Add a cup of marrow water.

Place the heatproof bowl with the marrow in a steamer, and steam vigorously for 30 minutes. Garnish with chopped ham and bring the marrow bowl to the table. Serve the contents with a silver spoon or ladle.

Autumn on the East River (Tiuchow)

Abalone, Fish and Prawn Balls
Braised Beef Balls

Pork Trotter Jelly
Carp wrapped in Lotus Leaf.
Liver and Kidney Buried in Salt
Eight Treasures Chicken
Egg and Tripe with Salted Cabbage

ABALONE, FISH AND PRAWN BALLS

1 can abalone (8–10 oz.)
4 oz. shrimps or prawns
4 oz. fish (cod, halibut, carp, haddock, bream, etc.)
2 oz. pork fat
1 lightly beaten egg
3 tablespoons cornflour
2 oz. ham
2 oz. parsley
¾ pint chicken broth
½ teaspoon M.S.G.
½ teaspoon salt
1 slice root ginger
1 tablespoon sherry

Chop the abalone, shrimps and fish and pound into a fine paste. Chop pork fat coarsely. Mix them together in a basin with beaten egg and cornflour.

Form the mixture into balls about half the size of hen's eggs.

Mince the ham and the parsley and keep separate. Dip one side of each ball in the minced ham, and the other in the minced parsley. Put the balls in a deep heatproof dish in a steamer and steam vigorously for 20 minutes.

Meanwhile, heat the chicken broth in a small pan, add M.S.G., salt, ginger and sherry and simmer for 3 minutes. Pour the broth over the fish balls, and bring the dish to the table. This is not exactly a soup in the normal western sense, but a semi-soup which, like all Chinese soups, is kept on the table throughout the meal.

BRAISED BEEF BALLS

1 lb. braising beef
1 teaspoon salt
2 oz. pork fat
2 oz. water chestnuts
1 egg (lightly beaten)
2 tablespoons cornflour
3 medium onions
2 tablespoons vegetable oil
1½ tablespoons soya sauce
1½ teaspoons sugar
6 tablespoons chicken broth
½ teaspoon M.S.G.
pepper

Mince the beef and pound it to a paste in a mortar. Chop pork fat and water chestnut coarsely. Mix them all together in a basin with beaten egg, salt and cornflour. Form them into balls about the size of chestnuts.

Drop the balls in boiling water to simmer for 10 minutes (or until they rise to the surface). Remove and drain.

Meanwhile, chop the onions and fry in oil for 2 minutes, then add sugar, soya sauce, chicken broth and M.S.G. Lower the heat and stir-fry for 1 minute. Add the beef balls to the frying-pan; turn them a few times in the onion and gravy, sprinkle with pepper, cover and leave to cook over low heat for 2 minutes. Serve in a warmed dish, surrounding the pile of onion at the centre of the dish with beef balls.

PORK TROTTER JELLY

2 lb. pork trotters (about 6 trotters)
6 oz. belly pork
3 oz. pork skin
3 tablespoons shrimp sauce
3 teaspoons brown sugar
2 slices root ginger
3 tablespoons dry sherry
1 tablespoon light soya sauce

Clean trotters thoroughly. Cut the belly pork into four pieces. Boil the meat and trotters and pork skin in a pan of water for 10 minutes. Pour away the water.

Arrange the pork trotters and skin at the bottom of a heavy iron pot.

Add sugar, shrimp sauce and ginger and pour in 2 pints of water. Bring to boil and leave to simmer over very low heat for 2½ hours. (Put an asbestos sheet under the pot.)

Gently remove the trotters and pork, which should now be very tender, and arrange them in a large serving bowl. Discard the pork skin and ginger. Add sherry, soya sauce, and M.S.G. to the liquid in the pot. Bring to boil gently, and simmer for a couple of minutes. Pour this sauce over the trotters and pork through a fine sieve. When the contents of the bowl have cooled, place in a refrigerator for 3 hours to jellify.

The meat jelly and tender trotters and pork make an exceptionally appetizing accompaniment to hot boiled rice, or *congee* (rice porridge eaten by the poor in China, or as a breakfast dish). Half dig the pieces of meat out of the jelly to serve. The dish can be kept in the refrigerator for 5–6 days.

CARP WRAPPED IN LOTUS LEAF

2 tablespoons vegetable oil
2 oz. bamboo-shoots (diced into ¼ in. pieces)
4 tablespoons Chinese mushrooms (soaked and diced)
4 oz. Cantonese roast pork (see p. 94)
2 oz. bacon (cut in strips)
3 spring onions (in 2 in. segments)
3 teaspoons sugar
3 slices root ginger (chopped)
2 tablespoons dried shrimps (soaked for 15 minutes)
1 tablespoon soya sauce
1 carp (3–4 lb.)
1½ teaspoons salt
1½ tablespoons cornflour

1 or 2 large sheets of lotus leaf
1½ pints chicken broth
1 teaspoon M.S.G.
2 tablespoons dry sherry

Heat oil in a frying-pan. Add bamboo-shoots, mushrooms, roast pork, bacon and onion. Stir-fry for 2 minutes. Add sugar, ginger, shrimps and soya sauce, and continue to stir-fry for 1 minute. Stuff the cavity of the carp with this mixture. Rub the outside of the fish with a mixture of salt and cornflour. Place the fish in a wire basket and lower it into hot oil in a deep-fryer to fry for 2½ minutes. Remove and drain.

Now wrap the fish up securely in the lotus leaf or leaves. If necessary secure with needle and thread. Heat the broth in a large saucepan, or fish kettle. Lower the carp into it and simmer gently for 25 minutes, turning it over once. Remove the fish from the kettle and unwrap it, discarding the lotus leaf. Place the fish on a deep oval dish. Add M.S.G. and sherry to half the sauce in the kettle (keep rest of sauce for other uses). Adjust seasoning, adding some soya sauce if required. Bring the sauce to the boil, pour it over the fish, and serve.

This might also be called a semi-soup. The lotus leaf both holds the fish together while it is cooking as well as adding its unique flavour.

LIVER AND KIDNEY BURIED IN SALT

8 oz. pig's liver
4 oz. lamb's kidney
2 medium onions (chopped)
2 slices root ginger (chopped)
3 tablespoons dry sherry
1½ lb. coarse sea salt

Clean liver and kidney thoroughly, and remove any gristle. Mix the onion, ginger and sherry. Marinate the kidney and

liver in the mixture for 2 hours (turning every half hour).
Remove them from the marinade and place in an airy place to
dry.

Heat the salt in a casserole over a low fire for 5 minutes,
turning it a few times. When the kidney and liver are quite
dry, bury them completely in the salt. Place the casserole in
an oven heated to 350°F, gas 4, for 45 minutes.

Uncover the kidney and liver and shake them free of salt.
Slice them thinly and arrange them in fish-scale fashion in
three rows, with the kidney in the middle row. (This dish can
be produced – on a smaller scale using chicken liver and kidney – for breakfast or a midnight supper to go with soft rice.)

Provided the liver and kidney are both quite dry before
they are buried in the salt, and provided coarse sea salt is
used, this dish will not be too salty.

EIGHT TREASURES CHICKEN

1 chicken (2–3 lb.)
2 tablespoons lard
4 oz. Cantonese roast pork (p. 94)
2 oz. lotus seeds (blanched)
6 Chinese dried mushrooms (soaked in water and stems removed)
1 oz. dried shrimps (soaked in water for half an hour and drained)
1 oz. dried squid (soaked in warm water for half an hour, drained and
   diced)
2 oz. chestnuts (blanched and chopped)
1 oz. smoked ham (diced)
1 oz. glutinous rice (soaked in warm water for half an hour and
   drained)
1½ teaspoons salt

Clean the chicken thoroughly inside and out.

Stir-fry all the other ingredients together in lard over moderate heat for 7—8 minutes.

Stuff the chicken with this mixture and sew up securely.
Place the chicken in a steamer and steam vigorously for half
an hour, and gently for another 45 minutes.

Chop the chicken into 10 pieces. Pile the stuffing in the centre of a warmed dish. Arrange the body of the chicken on top of the stuffing with the legs and wings around it, and serve. Eat dipped in high-quality soya sauce, soya-sherry mix, or soya-mustard mix (see p. 239).

EGG AND TRIPE WITH SALTED CABBAGE

8 eggs
6 oz. pig's tripe
2 tablespoons lard
1 medium onion (sliced)
2 oz. salted cabbage
2 oz. Chinese salami
4 large mushrooms (soaked and sliced into quarters)
2 tablespoons sherry
2 tablespoons soya sauce
1 teaspoon M.S.G.
6 tablespoons chicken broth

Hard-boil the eggs and remove shells. Slice tripe into 2 in. × ½ in. strips.

Heat lard in frying-pan. When hot, stir-fry onion in it for 1 minute. Add tripe and stir-fry for 1½ minutes. Add cabbage, sausage (cut diagonally to a thickness of ½–¾ in.), mushrooms and stir-fry together for another 1½ minutes. Add the eggs, pour the sherry and soya sauce over them, and sprinkle with M.S.G. Turn them under the other ingredients in the pan. Add chicken broth, cover and leave to cook for 2 minutes over moderate heat. To serve, arrange the eggs in the middle of the dish and surround them with cabbage, tripe, salami and mushrooms.

This is very much a local dish not often seen elsewhere in the country. It is an excellent accompaniment to rice for a meal at home.

Two of the favourite dips of Tiuchow, not often used elsewhere in China, are tangerine juice mixed in equal proportions with olive oil to make a dressing, and vinegar dip: two tablespoons of red wine vinegar are mixed with 1 teaspoon chilli oil and 2 tablespoons salad oil.

Winter in Foochow

Foochow Fish Soup
Steamed Pork in Ground Rice
Quick-fried Squid with Minced Meat
Quick-fried Duck in Red Wine Sediment Paste
Prawns on the Snow Mountain
Quick-braised Oyster on Toasted Bean Curd
Quick-fried Pig's Kidney in Sesame Sauce

FOOCHOW FISH SOUP

6 dried mushrooms (soaked for 20 minutes, stems removed and quartered)
½ lb. fish (cod, carp, mullet, bream, haddock or halibut)
2 oz. smoked ham
3 stalks celery
2 oz. carrots
1 egg
1½ tablespoons lard
1 onion (sliced)
2 thin slices root ginger
1 oz. salted cabbage (chopped)
2 pints chicken broth (or high broth p. 90)
1 teaspoon salt
2 tablespoons vinegar
1 tablespoon cornflour (blended in 3 tablespoons water)
1 tablespoon light soya sauce
pinch of pepper
1 teaspoon sesame oil

Cut fish into 1 in. cubes. Slice ham into 1 in. squares. Cut celery into 1 in. lengths and carrots into thin slices. Beat the eggs in a bowl for 10 seconds.

Heat lard in a saucepan. Add onion, carrot, ginger and celery and stir-fry for 2½ minutes. Add ham, salted cabbage and mushrooms. Continue to stir-fry for 1½ minutes. Pour in the broth, add salt, bring to the boil and simmer gently for 5 minutes. Add the pieces of fish and simmer for a further 5 minutes.

Add beaten egg trailing it in along the prongs of a fork.

Pour in vinegar, cornflour and soya sauce. Stir and bring to the boil again. Pepper lightly, add sesame oil and pour into a large tureen.

This is a piquant, warming, but light soup very suitable for the winter.

STEAMED PORK IN GROUND RICE

2½ lb. belly pork
3 tablespoons soya sauce
2 tablespoons dry sherry
chilli powder (to taste)
2 teaspoons sugar
3 oz. coarse rice

Remove the skin from the pork. Cut the meat into 1½ in. squares through the layers of lean and fat. Mix soya sauce, sherry, sugar and chilli together. Turn the pork in the mixture and leave in an airy place, first to marinate and then to dry, for 2 hours.

Heat the ground rice in a dry pan over low heat. Stir until it turns slightly brown and aromatic. Moisten the pieces of pork with what is left of the marinade and then turn them in the ground rice until every piece is well coated.

Place the pork in a heatproof bowl in a steamer, and steam vigorously for 1¼ hours. Serve in the bowl.

QUICK-FRIED SQUID WITH MINCED MEAT

½ lb. squid
3 tablespoons salt
2 tablespoons lard
2 tablespoons minced onion
1 clove garlic (crushed)
¼ lb. lean pork (minced)
4 large dried mushrooms (soaked, stems removed and minced)
2 teaspoons sugar
1½ tablespoons light soya sauce
2½ tablespoons dry sherry
few drops chilli oil
3 teaspoons tomato purée
4 tablespoons high broth (p. 90)
3 teaspoons cornflour (blended in 2 tablespoons water)
2 teaspoons sesame oil

Remove the head of the squid and the transparent backbone and clean. Immerse in brine (3 tablespoons salt in 2 pints water) for 2 hours. Bring the brine and squid to boil for 5 minutes. Rinse and soak the squid in fresh water for 5 minutes. Cut into 2½ in. × 1 in. strips. Make a few criss-cross cuts across one side of each piece.

Heat lard in a frying-pan. Add onion and garlic and stir-fry for 1 minute over high heat. Add pork and mushrooms and continue to stir-fry for 3 minutes. Add sugar, soya sauce, sherry, chilli oil, tomato purée and broth. When the mixture boils again, add the cornflour and stir. As soon as it thickens put in the pieces of squid. Turn them over a number of times – still over high heat – until all the squid is well covered with sauce. Add the sesame oil and turn out on to a warmed dish and serve. A good dish to accompany drinks.

QUICK-FRIED DUCK IN RED WINE SEDIMENT PASTE

1 duck (3–4 lbs.)
4 tablespoons chopped leeks
2 slices root ginger

1 clove garlic (chopped)
4 tablespoons red wine sediment paste (see p. 165)
½ tablespoon sugar
1½ teaspoons salt
½ teacup chicken broth
2½ tablespoons soya sauce
½ teacup sherry
1 tablespoon cornflour (blended in 3 tablespoons water)
oil for deep-frying

Chop duck through bone into pieces about 1½ ins.–2 ins. Heat oil in deep-fryer and fry the pieces of duck in it for 3 minutes. Drain and put aside.

Heat 2 tablespoons oil in a large frying-pan (with lid). Add leek, garlic, and ginger and stir-fry for ½ minute. Add wine sediment paste and sugar, and stir-fry together with the leek and garlic. Add the pieces of duck and salt and stir-fry over high heat for 5 minutes. Pour in the broth, sherry and soya sauce. Bring to boil and simmer, covered, for 20 minutes, turning the duck over a few times. Thicken with cornflour over high heat, turn duck over a few times and serve in a deep dish.

PRAWNS ON THE SNOW MOUNTAIN

6 oz. fresh peeled prawns
10 egg whites
2 teaspoons cornflour
½ teaspoon salt
1 teaspoon M.S.G.
1 oz. minced smoked ham
2 tablespoons chopped coriander leaves (or parsley or chives)
oil for deep-frying

Mix salt, cornflour and 1 egg white into a smooth paste. Turn the prawns in the paste. Place in a wire basket and deep-fry in hot oil for 1 minute. Drain and put aside.

Beat the remaining egg whites with M.S.G. until quite stiff.

Place half the egg white on a dish. Lay the prawns evenly over it. Fold the remaining egg whites over the prawns. Gently lower the prawns encased in egg-white into a pan of boiling oil and baste with oil for three minutes. Remove and drain. Sprinkle the top with chopped ham and coriander leaves (parsley or chives).

This is a colourful and interesting dish, good to serve with drinks; you have to dig for the prawns in the snow!

QUICK-BRAISED OYSTERS ON TOASTED BEAN CURD

2 onions (sliced)
1 tablespoon salt
½ lb. oysters (without shells)
3 bean curd cakes
oil for deep-frying
2 tablespoons chopped leek
1 clove garlic (chopped)
1½ tablespoons light soya sauce
1 teaspoon dry mustard
2 tablespoons dry sherry
6 tablespoons high broth (p. 90)
3 teaspoons cornflour (blended in 3 tablespoons water)

Boil onions and salt in 1 pint of water for 3 minutes. Simmer the oysters in the same water for 1½ minutes and drain, discarding onion and water. Cut each bean curd cake into 6 pieces.

Heat oil in the deep-fryer. When hot, deep-fry the pieces of bean curd for 3 minutes. Drain and arrange evenly in a single layer on a serving dish and keep warm.

Heat 2 tablespoons oil in a frying-pan. Add leek and garlic and stir-fry for 1 minute. Add soya sauce, mustard, sherry and broth. Stir until the mixture boils. Pour in the cornflour mixture, and stir until the sauce thickens. Add the oysters.

Stir gently for 1 minute. Pour the oysters and sauce over the bean curd and serve.

This is an exceptionally delicious dish, little known outside the province.

QUICK-FRIED PIG'S KIDNEY IN SESAME SAUCE

1 lb. pig's kidney
4 tablespoons sesame jam (or peanut butter blended with 1 tablespoon salad oil and 2 teaspoons sesame oil)
1 tablespoon chopped chives
2 tablespoons soya sauce
2 tablespoons dry sherry
2 teaspoons sugar
1 drop chilli oil
6 tablespoons vegetable oil

Remove the membrane from the kidney. Cut off all the gristle and tubes. Slice each kidney into four, lengthwise. Immerse them in fresh water for 15 minutes, and then dip them in boiling salted water (1 tablespoon salt in 1 pint water) for 1½ minutes. Remove, drain and dry with absorbent paper.

Mix sesame jam (or peanut butter and sesame oil), chopped chives, soya sauce, sherry, sugar, and chilli oil to a smooth consistency.

Heat oil in a frying-pan. When very hot put in the pieces of kidney. Stir-fry quickly but lightly for ½ minute. Ladle them on to a serving dish. Pour the sauce evenly over the kidneys and serve.

Seasons in North China

At the end of summer when we returned to Peking from the
south for the beginning of the university academic year, the
first thing we noticed as the train sped north from the banks
of the Yangtze was that the air got perceptibly less muggy.
Although the sun during the day was still hot, the evenings
were distinctly cool. Arriving in Peking on a September's
morning we noticed the stillness in the air, the deep shadows
in the courtyard, the timeless tranquillity in the quiet resi-
dences behind the high walls of the *hutungs* (city lanes), and
occasional lacquered doors.

Back in the capital, we repaired to our favourite eating
places and made pigs of ourselves. In Peking there were old
classical restaurants, which produced the dishes of the imperial kitchens, Moslem restaurants, 'earthen pot' (Chinese
Casserole) restaurants, restaurants specializing in crabs,
others in snacks, and all the different provincial restaurants,
Cantonese, Szechuanese, Shansi, Shantung, Foochow, all

with their provincial tastes and distinctive dishes: this makes Peking a culinary centre.

The brilliant autumn days were memorable, but soon over. Before long, the north wind blew, and suddenly we awoke one morning to find the lake and canal frozen over, and there were persimmons in the fruit stores. We used to put these fruit outside our windows at night, and the next day we made round holes in the top and scooped out the 'persimmon ice-cream' inside! These were quite a seasonal delight. Along the roadside the local restaurants and eating hovels, with their earthen floors, had already let down their heavy padded curtains to keep out the cold. Here the wealthier rickshaw pullers and local wide boys, and occasional suburban and village worthies gathered. Their favourite dishes were quick-fried mutton or lamb with large helpings of leeks, garlic and scallion (a kind of shallot), eaten with unleavened bread (called the 'big cake') or simply the standard north China steamed bread called *man-tou*.

For the young many of the favourite dishes in north China during the winter were of Moslem/Mongolian origins: thinly sliced lamb barbecued over open braziers, grilled and eaten with long chopsticks while standing up with one foot on the bench; or long-simmered soups, made in charcoal-burning Peking hot-pots.

After the long and freezing winter, the spring seemed to come very slowly to the north China plain; the seasonal wind blew for some time before finally the ice melted and the ground dried out after the thaw. One of the most refreshing snacks in the dusty northern spring was a spring roll, not the crisp pancake rolls of Chinese restaurants abroad, but the type which you wrapped yourself at the table using ready cooked pancakes. There was a type of vegetable called *chiu t'sai* with long stalks, tasting like a cross between chives and bean sprouts, which were fried with shredded pork or lamb, and brought steaming to the table for the customers to wrap for themselves into fat pancake rolls, thickly spread with various piquant sauces. The combination of meat with crunchy vegetables inside the rolls was delicious, and I seem to remember that we consumed them by the dozen!

The summers were hot, but not as long or as deadly as in the south. Sometimes it was humid and things grew mouldy; we cooled off by swimming in the Summer Palace Lake, which was not more than a couple of miles away. The bottom of the lake was overgrown with weeds and your feet got tangled in them. A better place to swim was the vast pool in the Nan Hai (South Sea) Park. After swimming, of course, we were starving again!

In the north in the summer, there seemed to be tomato in every other dish. Tomatoes were often cooked with beef, in soups, and in fried dishes, and sometimes prepared as a sweet, stuffed with dates. But one of the best things of the summer were the river crabs. There were a few restaurants which served nothing else. The crabs were simply steamed or boiled, and eaten dipped in ginger and vinegar. Everyone had a wooden hammer to crush the shells, and the pink and white meat was then sucked out. By the time you had had your fill the whole table top was piled high with a mountain of shells!

Along the coast lines of north China, in places like Pei-tai-Ho, Ching-wan-tao, Wei-hai-wei and Tsingtao, there were miles of golden sand and warm water, and fruit was plentiful: grapes, apples, peaches, plums, pomegranates and watermelons galore. One could live on them for days, as a break from the heavier, savoury foods. The blocks of ice which had been cut and stored in ice holes during the winter were now dug out for use in the summer.

For the gourmet autumn and winter were probably the most memorable seasons. Turned-out meats (the long-cooked, or long-steamed meat puddings flavoured with dried and salted vegetables and wine), turned out like a pudding on to a serving dish, were another favourite. Large prawns were also in season and were often dry-fried in their shells. Another unforgettable delight was Chinese cabbage (a kind of celery cabbage) either red-cooked (with soya sauce, wine, etc.) or white-cooked (with bone and chicken broth and flavoured with dried shrimps). Let me move on now from my memories to the actual recipes.

Peking in the Autumn

Jellied Chicken
Stuffed Eight-Treasure Tomatoes
Shredded Chicken in Mustard Sauce
Sliced Fish in White Wine sauce
Casserole of Lion's Head
Tungpo Mutton
Dry-fried Giant Prawns

JELLIED CHICKEN

4 oz. pork skin
3 chicken breasts (about 12 oz.)
2 oz. smoked ham (sliced)
1½ pints chicken broth (or high broth, see p. 90)
1 teaspoon salt
3 spring onions (thickly sliced)
2 slices root ginger
½ teaspooon M.S.G. (or 1 chicken stock cube)
3 tablespoons dry sherry
½ tablespoon gelatine (softened in water)
1 tablespoon chopped chives

Boil pork skin in a pint of water for 10 minutes. Drain and scrape it clean of fat.

T–F

Place pork skin at the bottom of a heavy saucepan. Cover it with the chicken. Pour in the broth until it covers the pork and chicken. Add ham, salt, onion and ginger. Bring the contents gently to the boil. Skim off impurities and simmer gently for 1½ hours.

Add sherry, M.S.G. and gelatine. Stir and remove from fire.

Use a pair of chopsticks or a perforated spoon to remove onion, ginger, ham, and pork skin. Spread the chicken out on a large, deep dish. Pour in the broth. When cool, place in a refrigerator for 3 hours to jellify.

To serve, cut each breast into 4–5 slices, and arrange on a flat dish. Chop the jelly and pile it evenly on top. Sprinkle with chopped chives and serve. In China it is eaten with hot rice but in the West it can be used as an hors d'oeuvre or a cold buffet dish.

STUFFED EIGHT-TREASURE TOMATOES

1½ oz. chopped cooked chicken meat
1½ oz. fish, filleted and chopped (haddock, cod, halibut)
1½ oz. smoked ham (chopped)
2 tablespoons dried mushrooms (soaked for 15 minutes, stems removed and diced)
1 slice root ginger (finely chopped)
1 clove garlic (crushed)
1 tablespoon chicken fat
6 large firm tomatoes
1 tablespoon vegetable oil
2 oz. cauliflower (in flowerets)
2 oz. cucumber (in ¼ in. slices)
pinch of salt
1 teacup high broth (p. 90)
½ teaspoon M.S.G.
2 teaspoons cornflour (blended in 2 tablespoons water)

Mix chicken meat, chopped fish, ham, diced mushrooms,

ginger and garlic to a paste with the chicken fat for use as filling.

Dip tomato in boiling water for a few seconds and remove skin. Cut a slice from the top of each tomato as a lid. Cut a hole at the centre, about three quarters of the way through, and remove the core and seeds. Stuff the cavity with prepared filling. Arrange the tomatoes on a heatproof dish and place in a steamer with their lids beside them, to steam for 15 minutes.

Meanwhile, heat vegetable oil in a frying-pan. When hot, stir-fry cauliflower and cucumber in it for 2 minutes. Add any extra filling, salt and broth, turn the contents over a few times, and simmer for 3 minutes. Add M.S.G. and cornflour. Stir a few more times.

Lift out the cauliflower and cucumber and place them around the tomatoes. Replace the lids on top of each tomato. Pour the thickened broth in the frying pan over the top of each tomato and serve.

SHREDDED CHICKEN IN MUSTARD SAUCE

10 oz. chicken breast
2 egg whites
1 tablespoon cornflour
2 tablespoons vegetable oil

mustard sauce

3 teaspoons dry mustard
¼ teaspoon salt
2 tablespoons soya sauce
1 teaspoon sugar
1 tablespoon vinegar
2 tablespoons chicken broth
1 tablespoon olive oil
½ teaspoon sesame oil

Cut the chicken meat into matchstick strips. Beat egg whites for 15 seconds, stir in shredded chicken. Sprinkle evenly with cornflour and mix well.

Heat the vegetable oil gently in a frying-pan; when hot, add the shredded chicken. Spread it out, cook lightly for 2 minutes. Arrange it in a small mound on a well-heated dish. Mix the mustard sauce by beating the rest of the ingredients together for 5 seconds and pour it over the pile of shredded chicken.

SLICED FISH IN WHITE WINE SAUCE

1 lb. very fresh fillet of fish (carp, bream, halibut, sole)
1 egg white
1½ tablespoons cornflour
1½ tablespoons lard
6 tablespoons dry white wine
½ teaspoon salt
1 teaspoon sugar
1 tablespoon cornflour (blended with 6 tablespoons concentrated chicken broth)
oil for deep-frying

Cut the fish into 2 in. × 1 in. slices. Rinse and dry thoroughly.

Dip the slices of fish in lightly beaten egg white and coat evenly with 1½ tablespoons cornflour.

Place the floured fish in a wire basket and lower it into the hot oil in the deep-fryer; fry for just under 1 minute over moderate heat.

Drain the fish. Melt the lard in a frying-pan, add sugar and wine. Stir well, then add the cornflour–chicken broth mixture. Tilt the pan, so that the fat and liquid run evenly over the bottom. Stir until sauce thickens. Now place the pieces of fish in the sauce. Turn them over a couple of times with a fish slice. Heat for ½ minute and the dish is ready to serve.

This dish is white and glistening and looks very attractive.

CASSEROLE OF LION'S HEAD

1¼ lb. lean pork
3 tablespoons soya sauce
3 tablespoons dry sherry
1½ teaspoons salt
2 medium onions (finely chopped)
2 cloves garlic (crushed)
2 slices root ginger (finely chopped)
1½ tablespoons cornflour
½ lb. spinach
2 tablespoons lard
oil for deep-frying

'Lion's Head' is the traditional name for large meat balls on a spinach base.

Chop and mince the pork coarsely. Mix it in a basin with 1 tablespoon soya sauce, half the sherry, half the salt, onion, garlic and ginger and all the cornflour. Form the mixture into 4 large meat balls.

Lower them in a wire basket into hot oil in a deep-fryer for just 2½ minutes. Remove, drain, and place them at the bottom of a casserole. Pour in ½ pint water and add the remainder of the soya sauce, onion, garlic, ginger. Place the casserole, covered, in an oven pre-heated to 350°F, gas 4, for 45 minutes. Clean the spinach thoroughly, and discard coarse stems. Heat lard in a large saucepan. When very hot add the spinach and remainder of the salt. Stir-fry for 2½ minutes. Remove the casserole from the oven. Put the spinach underneath the meat balls and add the remainder of the sherry.

Heat the casserole over moderate heat for 10 minutes and serve in the casserole.

Although this dish may seem rough and ready, it is surprisingly good and is sometimes used as a banquet dish.

TUNGPO MUTTON

3 lb. lean mutton
¼ lb. potatoes
¼ lb. carrots
1 large onion (sliced)
2 slices root ginger
1 clove garlic (crushed)
4 oz. leek (sliced)
1 teaspoon chilli sauce
4 tablespoons soya sauce
3 tablespoons sherry
2 teaspoons brown sugar
oil for deep-frying

Cut mutton into large slices about ½ in. thick. Cut each piece again diagonally into four, thus forming triangular pieces.

Peel potatoes and also cut into triangular, wedge-shaped pieces. Slice carrots diagonally.

Heat oil in deep-fryer. When hot, deep-fry the pieces of mutton in a wire basket for 3 minutes. Drain. Place the potatoes and carrots in the wire basket and deep-fry them for 3 minutes also and drain.

Now place the mutton in a heavy saucepan or iron pot. Add onion, garlic, ginger, leek, soya sauce, chilli sauce, sherry and brown sugar. Pour in 1 pint of water. Bring contents to the boil gently, and simmer for 1¾ hours. Finally add the carrots and potato, burying them under the mutton and heat together for 20 minutes. Serve in a deep dish. This is another rough and ready dish of provincial origin, notwithstanding its elegant name, Tungpo, which is the name of the famous Tang Dynasty poet.

DRY-FRIED GIANT PRAWNS

6 fresh giant prawns (or Pacific prawns) with shells
1 medium onion (sliced very finely)
3 slices ginger
2 cloves garlic (crushed)

2 tablespoons vegetable oil
2 tablespoons dry sherry
1 teaspoon sugar
¼ teaspoon salt
½ teaspoon M.S.G.
2 tablespoons chicken broth
1 tablespoon lard
1 spring onion or chives (chopped)

Clean prawns thoroughly, remove feelers and legs, and cut each prawn in two from head to tail, but do not remove the shell. Remove the dark vein from the back.

Heat oil in a frying-pan. Add onion, ginger, and garlic and stir-fry for 2 minutes. Add the prawns and stir-fry gently until they have turned red. Now add sherry, sugar, salt M.S.G. and broth. Simmer gently until almost all the liquid has evaporated. Sprinkle with chopped chives or spring onion, add lard and stir-fry gently together for another few seconds and serve.

Peking in the Winter

Hot and Sour Soup with Shrimps
Peking Casserole of Beef
Empress Meat Pudding in Soya and Herb Sauce
White Braised Cabbage
Fried Pig's Liver with Tree-fungi
Aromatic Crispy Duck
Kao Li Frosted Bean Paste Balls

HOT AND SOUR SOUP WITH SHRIMPS

2 bean curd cakes
2 oz. bamboo-shoots
4 Chinese dried mushrooms
1 medium onion (chopped)
1½ tablespoons lard

2 pints chicken broth
2 oz. fresh shrimps (shelled)
2 tablespoons soya sauce
1 chicken stock cube
3 tablespoons vinegar
¼ teaspoon black pepper
1½ tablespoons cornflour (blended in 3 tablespoons water)
1 egg
½ teaspoon sesame oil

Cut each bean curd cake into 8 squares. Cut bamboo-shoots into matchstick shreds. Soak the mushrooms in a cup of warm water for 15 minutes. Discard stalks, cut mushrooms into quarters and reserve the liquor.

Heat lard in a saucepan. When it has melted add bamboo-shoots, mushrooms, and onion and stir-fry for 2 minutes. Pour in the chicken broth and bring to boil. Add bean curd, shrimps and mushroom water. Bring to the boil again, then add soya sauce, stock cube, vinegar and pepper. Allow the soup to simmer for 3 minutes. Pour in the cornflour mixture to thicken.

Beat egg for 15 seconds in a bowl, and stream it into the soup very slowly along the prongs of a fork over the whole surface of the soup. Add sesame oil, stir and serve.

PEKING CASSEROLE OF BEEF

3 lb. stewing beef
2 teaspoons sugar
4 tablespoons soya sauce
4 tablespoons sherry
2 slices root ginger
2 medium onions (sliced)
1 tablespoon dried tangerine peel
oil for deep-frying

Cut beef into 1 in. squares. Deep-fry for 3—3½ minutes. Drain, place in a large saucepan and cover with boiling water.

Bring to the boil and keep boiling for 2 minutes. Pour away the water and transfer the beef to a casserole. Add sugar, soya sauce, sherry, ginger, onion, tangerine peel and 1½ pints fresh water.

Close the lid of the casserole. Place in a pre-heated oven at 375°F, gas 5, for half an hour. Reduce the heat to 325°F, gas 3, for 4 hours. Turn the beef over gently every hour. When ready, the beef should be so tender that it practically disintegrates. Delicious with rice.

EMPRESS MEAT PUDDING IN SOYA AND HERB SAUCE

3 lb. belly pork in one piece
4 tablespoons soya sauce
3 tablespoons dry sherry
½ cup chicken broth
½ teaspoon M.S.G.
3 teaspoons cornflour (blended in 2 tablespoons water)

for the soya and herb sauce

1½ pints water
1 teacup soya sauce
5 oz. ordinary or crystal sugar
2 cloves garlic (crushed)
2 slices root ginger
1 anise star
1 large onion (sliced)
bouquet garni

To prepare the sauce, heat water in a saucepan. Add soya sauce and sugar; put the ginger, garlic, anise star, onion and bouquet garni in a muslin bag and drop in. Bring the contents to boil, and simmer for half an hour.

Remove the bag, and the sauce is ready for use. Put pork into a pan of boiling water and continue to boil for 10 minutes. Cool slightly and cut the pork through the skin into 4 pieces. Simmer the pieces in the sauce for 25 minutes, when they will have turned quite brown. Remove pork from sauce and cut each piece into 6 pieces, again through the skin. Reserve sauce in the refrigerator for another occasion.

Pack the pieces of pork, skin side down, in a heatproof bowl. Sprinkle with half the soya sauce and half the sherry. Place in a steamer and steam vigorously for 45 minutes.

Meanwhile heat the rest of the soya sauce and sherry, the chicken broth and M.S.G. in a small saucepan. Add cornflour and stir until sauce thickens. When the pork is ready, turn it out on to a warmed, deep serving dish, skin side up. Pour the sauce over it and serve.

WHITE BRAISED CABBAGE

1 large Chinese cabbage (or a 2–3 lb. Savoy cabbage)
2 tablespoons vegetable oil
1 teaspoon salt
2 slices root ginger
1 tablespoon dried shrimps
½ cup chicken broth (strengthened with ½ chicken stock cube)
½ cup white broth (made by boiling some bones vigorously for 2 hours – or use milk with 2 tablespoons cream and 4 tablespoons chicken broth added)
2 tablespoons cornflour
½ teaspoon M.S.G.
2 tablespoons dry white wine

Clean cabbage thoroughly and remove coarse outer leaves. Cut into quarters and then cut each quarter in half.

Heat oil in a saucepan. Add cabbage, sprinkling it with salt. Turn the cabbage in the pan until the pieces are well oiled, without allowing them to break up. Add ginger and dried shrimps and pour in the concentrated chicken broth. Cover the contents and simmer gently for 15 minutes.

Mix together the M.S.G., cornflour and cold white broth or milk and pour over the cabbage pieces turning them with a metal spoon, so that the mixture is evenly dispersed. Add wine. Simmer cabbage and other ingredients together for another 5–6 minutes.

Turn the cabbage out on to a serving bowl, arranging it as nearly as possible into its original shape. Pour the remaining white sauce in the pan over the reassembled cabbage.

An extremely appetizing vegetable dish to eat with various brown meat dishes.

FRIED PIG'S LIVER WITH TREE-FUNGI

1 lb. pig's liver in slices ¼ in. × 2 in. × 1½ ins.
¾ oz. dried tree-fungi (soaked in warm water for 30 minutes, thoroughly cleaned)
10 oz. chicken breast
3 spring onions (in 2 in. segments)
2 tablespoons soya sauce
2 teaspoons sugar
3 teaspoons cornflour (blended in 2 tablespoons water)
1 tablespoon dry sherry
6 tablespoons vegetable oil

Heat 1½ tablespoons oil in a frying-pan. Add onion and stir-fry for 15 seconds. Add tree-fungi, sprinkle with salt, and, after stir-frying for 10 seconds, remove the fungi and put aside.

Add the remaining oil to the pan. When it is very hot spread the sliced liver over the base, turn and cook for ½ minute, remove with a perforated spoon and place at the bottom of a large basin. Pour in half a kettle of boiling water, completely covering the pieces of liver. Stir them with a pair of chopsticks. After 10 seconds pour away all the water, draining as completely as possible.

Now add sugar, soya sauce, sherry and cornflour to the basin; mix evenly with the liver.

Heat the oil in the frying-pan again, and pour the liver back. Stir-fry gently over high heat for 15 seconds. Add the tree-fungi. Turn them over with the liver three or four times. Lift them on to a serving dish with a perforated spoon, pour sauce over item. Serve immediately.

AROMATIC CRISPY DUCK

1 duckling (4–5 lb.)
Soya and herb sauce (see p. 153 make double portion)
vegetable oil for deep-frying
½ cucumber
10 spring onions

Cut spring onion and cucumber into 2 in. segments.

Clean duck thoroughly. Immerse in a panful of boiling water and simmer for 10 minutes. Drain.

Heat the soya and herb sauce in a large pan and when it starts to boil, put in the duck and simmer for 30 minutes. It will turn very brown and aromatic. Drain thoroughly.

Shortly before serving, heat the oil in the deep-fryer until a bread crumb will sizzle in it. Lower the duck into the oil in a wire basket. Cover and allow it to deep-fry for 10 minutes, or until the skin of the duck is quite crisp.

Drain and bring to the table in a hot serving dish. Loosen the flesh and skin of the duck with a knife.

The duck meat and skin should be eaten with steamed buns (see pp. 232–3) in sandwich fashion, together with a strip or two of cucumber and spring onion. Plum sauce, tomato-soya sauce, or soya-chilli sauce as dips should be placed in small saucers around the table.

KAO LI FROSTED BEAN PASTE BALLS (Sweetened bean paste meringue balls)

1½ tablespoons lard
4 oz. sweetened bean paste (see pp. 157 and 242)
5 egg whites
1 tablespoon flour

1 tablespoon cornflour
1 tablespoon caster sugar
2 tablespoons sugar
vegetable oil for deep-frying

Stir-fry bean paste in hot lard for 2 minutes over moderate heat. When cool, form the bean paste into round balls the size of small chestnuts.

Meanwhile, whip egg whites for 1 minute or so until quite stiff. Fold in flour, cornflour, and caster sugar and beat them together.

Coat the bean paste balls thickly with this meringue.

Heat vegetable oil in a large frying-pan. When very hot, add the balls, three or four at a time, and fry for 2 minutes.

Drain them on a sheet of absorbent paper, arrange on a warmed dish, sprinkle with sugar and serve. (Alternatively, the meringue balls can be placed on a heatproof dish in a preheated oven at 400°F, gas 6, for 10 minutes.)

Note: Sweetened red bean paste is made by boiling Chinese red beans for 1 hour in enough water to just cover. Transfer to a blender and blend at high speed. Drain off the water through a cheese cloth. Add sugar and peanut oil, approximately ¼ as much sugar and ⅛ as much oil or lard to the mash in a thick-bottomed saucepan, and heat together with a small amount of water for 5–6 minutes, stirring all the time. A thick paste will result.

Hopei in the Spring

Shredded Chicken Soup
Quick-fried Fresh Shrimps
Quick-fried Cubed Chicken with Sweet and Chilli Pepper
Double-fried Bamboo-Shoots
Hot-fried Sliced Pork

Braised Triple White
Peas Quick-fried in Chicken Fat

Hopei is the province in which Peking is situated. *Ho* is Chinese for river, and *Pei* means north: in other words, 'north of the Yellow River'.

SHREDDED CHICKEN SOUP

4 oz. chicken breast
3 oz. bamboo-shoots
1 egg
2 teaspoons cornflour (blended in 2 teaspoons water)
1 lb. lard for deep-frying
1½ pints chicken broth
1 teaspoon salt
2 slices root ginger
½ teaspoon M.S.G.
3 teaspoons cornflour (blended in 6 teaspoons water)
1 teaspoon chicken fat

Cut the chicken with a very sharp knife into the thinnest possible slices. Place the slices on top of one another and cut into strips thinner than matchsticks. Cut bamboo-shoots similarly.

Beat egg for 10 seconds, add half of it to the shredded chicken, mix well and add the 2 teaspoons blended cornflour. Mix evenly, and spread out the shredded chicken.

Heat lard in a saucepan. When hot add the shredded chicken in a wire basket. Spread it out and give it just 5 seconds very quick frying. Remove from pan and drain off all the fat.

Meanwhile, heat the chicken broth in another pan. Add salt, ginger, M.S.G., and shredded bamboo-shoots. Bring to boil, skimming off scum. Simmer for 3 minutes. Add the 3 teaspoons blended cornflour. Finally scatter the shredded

chicken into the soup. As soon as it boils again, add chicken fat and serve.

QUICK-FRIED FRESH SHRIMPS

1½ lb. fresh shrimps

for marinade

2 tablespoons dry sherry
1 teaspoon salt
1 egg white

for cooking

1 slice root ginger (finely chopped)
½ teaspoon salt
½ teaspoon M.S.G.
1 tablespoon dry sherry
6 tablespoons vegetable oil

Wash the shrimps thoroughly in their shells with two changes of water, and then remove the shells. Combine the marinade ingredients, and put the shrimps into it. Leave to stand for 10 minutes, then discard the marinade.

Heat oil in a frying-pan. When very hot add the shrimps and stir-fry for 15 seconds. Remove pan from the heat. Remove the shrimps and drain off all the oil.

Add the chopped ginger and salt to the oil remaining in the pan. Replace the pan on the fire, and stir-fry for 10 seconds. Return the shrimps to the pan. Sprinkle with M.S.G. and sherry. Stir-fry again for 15 seconds. Serve on a hot dish.

The shrimps should be reddish-pink in colour and very fresh and tasty.

QUICK-FRIED CUBED CHICKEN WITH
SWEET PEPPER AND CHILLI PEPPER

10 oz. chicken breast
2 green or red sweet peppers

2 green chilli peppers
2 tablespoons soya sauce
1 tablespoon cornflour (blended with 1½ tablespoons water)
1 tablespoon vinegar
2 tablespoons chicken broth
1 teaspoon sesame oil
6 tablespoons vegetable oil

Dice chicken meat into ¼ in. cubes. Cut sweet pepper and chilli pepper into ¾ in.–½ in. squares.

Add the blended cornflour and 1 tablespoon soya sauce to the chicken and mix well.

Heat oil in a frying-pan. When hot add the chicken cubes and stir-fry briskly for 10 seconds. Remove, drain and pour off most of the oil.

Place the pan over the fire again. Add sweet pepper and chilli pepper. Stir-fry them for ½ minute in the remaining oil in the pan. Return the chicken cubes to the pan. Add the remaining soya sauce, vinegar and chicken broth. Stir-fry briskly for 15 seconds. Sprinkle with sesame oil, check seasoning and serve.

DOUBLE-FRIED BAMBOO-SHOOTS

1½ lb. bamboo-shoots
1 tablespoon lard
½ oz. Szechuan pickled cabbage (finely chopped)
1 slice root ginger (finely chopped)
3 teaspoons oyster sauce
1½ tablespoons soya sauce
2 tablespoons dry sherry
4 tablespoons chicken broth
2 teaspoons sugar
1 teaspoon sesame oil
1 teaspoon M.S.G.
vegetable oil for deep-frying

If using fresh bamboo-shoots, remove outer leaves and coarser roots. Cut them into wedge-shaped pieces (½ in. thick at the thicker edge).

Heat oil in a deep-fryer. When very hot, fry the bamboo-shoots for 2 minutes. Lower the heat to medium low and continue to fry for 2 more minutes. Remove and drain.

Heat lard in a frying-pan. When hot add the ginger, Szechuan cabbage, and finally the fried bamboo-shoots. Add soya sauce, oyster sauce, chicken broth, sherry, sugar and M.S.G. and turn the heat up to the maximum. Stir-fry for ½ minute. Sprinkle with sesame oil and serve in a hot dish.

HOT-FRIED SLICED PORK

1½ lb. belly pork
3 young leeks
2 red chilli peppers
2½ tablespoons vegetable oil
2 teaspoons salted beans (soaked in water for 10 minutes, drained and chopped)
2 teaspoons soya bean paste
¼ teaspoon salt
1 tablespoon soya sauce
2 teaspoons sugar
3 tablespoons sherry

Remove skin from the pork, and cut across lean and fat into 1½ in. × 1 in. slices. Cut leeks diagonally into ½ in. segments, and chilli peppers into ¼ in. segments, after removing all the seeds.

Heat oil in a large frying-pan. When very hot, put in the pork and salt. Stir-fry briskly for 5 minutes. Add salted beans and stir-fry for 10 seconds. Then add bean paste and chilli peppers and stir-fry for another 10 seconds. Then add soya sauce, sherry and sugar. After 20 seconds stir-frying, still over high heat, add the young leeks. Stir-fry more gently now for 1 minute and serve.

This is a straightforward dish given a lot of kick by the chilli pepper.

BRAISED TRIPLE WHITE

4 oz. chicken breast
4 oz. celery (Chinese celery cabbage if available)
4 oz. asparagus
1½ tablespoons lard
1 medium onion (sliced)
2 slices root ginger
6 tablespoons high broth (p. 90)
3 tablespoons white wine
½ teaspoon salt
½ teaspoon M.S.G.
1 tablespoon cornflour (blended in 3 tablespoons water)
6 tablespoons milk
1½ tablespoons chicken fat

Cut chicken thinly into 1½ in. × 1 in. pieces. Clean thoroughly. Remove the tougher parts of asparagus and clean thoroughly. Cut the celery and the asparagus diagonally across into 2½–3 in. lengths. Parboil the celery and asparagus for 6 minutes and drain. Place all three items separately on a plate.

Heat lard in a frying pan. When fairly hot, add onion and ginger. Stir-fry gently for 1 minute. Pour in the broth and wine. Stir a few times. Remove and discard the onion and ginger. Now slide the three whites: chicken, asparagus, and celery into the pan. Sprinkle with salt, and M.S.G. Bring to the boil again, and cover and simmer for 1 minute. Turn contents over once and simmer for another minute.

Blend the cornflour mixture thoroughly with the milk. Stream the mixture evenly into the pan. Spread about a third of the chicken fat round the pan. Turn the contents over once with the help of a fish slice or spatula. Sprinkle with remaining chicken fat and serve.

PEAS QUICK-FRIED IN CHICKEN FAT

1¼ lb. fresh green peas (shelled or frozen peas)
4 tablespoons chicken broth
2 tablespoons dry sherry
1 teaspoon salt
3 tablespoons chicken fat
2 teaspoons sugar

Heat fat in a frying-pan. When hot add the peas. Turn and stir-fry slowly for 2 minutes over medium heat. Add chicken broth and continue to stir-fry for 1 more minute. Sprinkle with salt, sugar and sherry and stir-fry gently for 1 further minute and serve. An excellent plain dish to serve with more elaborate dishes.

Summer in Shantung

Liver and Tripe Soup
Steamed Pork with Wine Sediment Paste
Shredded Kidney with Mustard and Chilli Dressing
Sweet and Sour whole Carp
Fu-Yung Crab
Quick-fried Bean Sprouts
Lotus Root Custard

Shantung means east of the mountain, from *Shan* – Chinese for mountain – and *Tung*, the word for east. Shantung is, in fact, a peninsula jutting out into the North China Sea. In the western part of the province there is a mountain called Tai-shan, which rises to about 5,000 feet; around this mountain the great sages Confucius and Mencius lived and worked during the fourth and fifth centuries before Christ.

LIVER AND TRIPE SOUP

4 oz. pig's tripe
3 oz. chicken liver
2 tablespoons salt
1 tablespoon vinegar
2 tablespoons dry sherry
1 tablespoon soya sauce
good pinch black pepper
1 tablespoon lard
1 tablespoon chopped onion
4 young leeks
1 slice root ginger
2 pints high broth (see p. 90)
1 teaspoon salt
½ teaspoon M.S.G. (or ½ teaspoon chicken stock cube)

Cut tripe into 1½ in. × ½ in. strips. Remove membrane, tubes, and gristle from the chicken liver. Cut into slices only ⅛ in. thick. Soak liver and tripe separately in two bowls of brine (1 tablespoon salt in ½ pint of water) for half an hour. Drain.

Heat a pan of water until boiling. Add the liver to the boiling water first, then the tripe. After 1½ minutes remove, drain and put in a large bowl. Add the vinegar and sherry, soya sauce and pepper and mix thoroughly.

Heat lard in another saucepan. When hot, add onion, leeks, and ginger and stir-fry for ½ minute. Add broth and salt and sprinkle with M.S.G. Simmer the soup for ½ minute. Pour the soup into the bowl containing the tripe and liver, and serve.

STEAMED PORK WITH WINE SEDIMENT PASTE

2 lb. belly pork
1 teaspoon salt
2 tablespoons soya sauce
2 tablespoons wine sediment paste (see Note: p. 165)

2 tablespoons dry sherry
2 tablespoons high broth (see p. 90)
2 teaspoons sugar
oil for deep-frying
2 tablespoons shredded onion
1 tablespoon shredded root ginger

Cut pork through the skin into 2 in. × 2½ in. × 1 in. pieces and rub with salt.

Mix soya sauce, wine sediment paste, broth, sugar and sherry in a bowl.

Heat oil in the deep-fryer. When quite hot, lower the pork in a wire basket and fry in the oil for 5 minutes. Remove and drain.

When it has cooled slightly, pack the pork, skin side down, in a heatproof bowl. Sprinkle the top of the pork evenly with shredded onion and ginger and the soya sauce mixture in the bowl. Place in a steamer and steam for 1½ hours. Serve in the original bowl. Delicious with rice.

Note: *Wine Sediment Paste.* An acceptable substitute for wine sediment paste can be prepared by mixing together 2 tablespoons chopped onion, 1 tablespoon soya bean paste, 1 tablespoon finely chopped orange peel, 1 teaspoon chopped garlic, 1 teaspoon finely chopped root ginger, 1 teaspoon ground rice, 2 teaspoons sugar, ½ teaspoon salt, 2 tablespoons tomato pureé and half a cup dry sherry. Heat gently until the sauce has reduced to about a quarter and the mixture has become a thick paste. Add 1 tablespoon brandy, and heat, stirring slowly for another 3 minutes.

SHREDDED KIDNEY WITH MUSTARD AND CHILLI DRESSING

1 lb. pig's kidney
4 oz. celery
1 teaspoon salt

for dressing

1 tablespoon chopped coriander leaves or parsley
3 tablespoons dry sherry
2 tablespoons soya sauce
2 tablespoons salad oil
1 teaspoon M.S.G.
2 teaspoons mustard powder
1 teaspoon chilli sauce

Remove membrane, tubes and gristle from the kidney. Slice with a sharp knife into 3–4 flat pieces and cut again into thin matchstick strips or shreds. Cut celery similarly. Soak kidney and celery in brine (1 tablespoon salt in 1 pint water) for 20 minutes. Rinse under running water, and stand them in a bowl of fresh water.

Beat the ingredients for the dressing together in a bowl until they are blended smoothly.

Drain the kidney and celery. Add them to a pan of boiling water. Stir and spread them out with a pair of chopsticks. Simmer them for 1 minute; remove and drain immediately, and arrange them on a serving dish. Pour the dressing over evenly and serve.

SWEET AND SOUR CARP

1 carp (2–3 lb.)
4 tablespoons flour
1 teaspoon salt
oil for deep-frying
2 tablespoons Chinese treefungi (soaked 20 minutes, cleaned and water discarded)
2 oz. bamboo-shoots (sliced to thickness of ⅙ in.)
2 oz. red pimento (sliced)
2 tablespoons oil

for sauce

½ teacup chicken broth
1½ tablespoons cornflour (blended in 3 tablespoons water)
1½ tablespoons soya sauce
1½ tablespoons sugar
1½ tablespoons wine vinegar
2 tablespoons dry sherry
2 teaspoons tomato purée
1 teaspoon chilli sauce
¼ teaspoon salt

Clean the carp thoroughly and scrape off the scales. Score the fish by making diagonal cuts 2 ins. × 2½ ins. long and ¼ in. deep at 1½ in. intervals on both sides of the fish (about half a dozen times along the length). Rub the fish with salt and then with flour.

Heat the oil in the deep-fryer. When very hot lower the fish into the oil to deep-fry for 6 minutes or until the outside of the fish starts to get brown and crisp. Drain and keep hot (in the oven).

Meanwhile, blend the ingredients for the sauce to a smooth consistency.

Heat 2 tablespoons oil in a frying-pan. Add tree fungi, bamboo-shoots and pimento, and quick-fry over moderate heat for 1½ minutes. Pour in the sauce mixture. Stir until the sauce thickens. Place the carp on a warmed oval dish, pour over the sweet and sour sauce and serve.

FU-YUNG CRAB

4 oz. crab (pink meat)
6 egg whites
6 tablespoons chicken broth
½ teaspoon salt
3 tablespoons lard
1 tablespoon chopped onion
1 clove garlic (crushed)
1 slice root ginger (chopped)

1 teaspoon sugar
2 tablespoons dry sherry

Beat egg whites, 2 tablespoons broth and ¼ teaspoon salt in a bowl for 1 minute.

Heat 1 tablespoon lard in a frying-pan. Add onion, garlic and ginger and stir-fry together for 1 minute. Add the crab and stir-fry together for another minute. Add sugar, sherry, the rest of the salt and broth. Stir-fry together gently for a further 2 minutes.

Meanwhile heat remainder of lard in another pan. When hot and the bottom of the pan is well covered with fat, pour in the egg-white mixture and stir quickly for 15 seconds, then pour in the crab mixture. Turn and scramble a few times and serve.

QUICK-FRIED BEAN SPROUTS

1¼ lb. fat bean sprouts
1 tablespoon chopped spring onion (or chives)
1 tablespoon chopped 'snow' pickled cabbage (obtainable from Chinese foodstores)
3 tablespoons chicken fat
1 teaspoon sesame oil
1 teaspoon salt
3 tablespoons chicken broth

Heat fat in a large saucepan over high heat. Add onion and pickled cabbage. Stir-fry for ½ minute. Pour in the bean sprouts. Turn and stir-fry briskly until all the sprouts are well coated with fat. Sprinkle the sprouts with salt. Continue to stir-fry for 1½ minutes. Add chicken broth and sesame oil, stir-fry for 1 further minute and serve.

LOTUS ROOT CUSTARD

1 lb. shredded fresh lotus roots (or pineapple)
2 oz. dates (shredded)

2 oz. crystallized fruit
1 oz. dried figs (shredded)
3 eggs
4 tablespoons sugar
1 breakfast cup water
1 tablespoon cornflour

Beat eggs in a bowl for 10 seconds. Add 1 tablespoon sugar and ¼ breakfast cup of water; beat together for 5 seconds. Pour the mixture into a dish 2 ins. deep. Place in a steamer and steam for 7–8 minutes until the egg has hardened.

Spread the shredded lotus roots (or pineapple) on top, and arrange the shredded dates, figs and crystallized fruit in separate piles in the middle.

Blend cornflour in the remaining ¾ cup of water together with remaining sugar. Heat the mixture, stirring until it thickens into a syrup. Pour this syrup over the dish and serve either hot or chilled.

Seasons In East China

Life in east China along the lower reaches of the Yangtse is much less austere than in the north. But contrary to expectations both the summer and winter are much more extreme than one might expect. One of the hottest nights I have ever experienced was in Nanking; and I will never forget the shock of the heat in Shanghai, where, emerging one day from an air-conditioned cinema, I saw the very asphalt on the street about to melt into black mud. Yet the winter was always freezing, and the wind biting, and we had to wrap up in thick coats and peep through scarves up to our eyes at the steel of the tram-rails glinting in the cold winter's sun. Neither the heat nor the cold was comfortable in this limbo of China. The average house had no heating system, unlike in the north, where even the peasants had their *kung* (the heated brick bed where the whole family slept); nor the tall roofs and stone-flagged floors of the south, which helped absorb some of the heat and allowed breezes to circulate in the hot summer. Friends who were studying at the Nanyang College of Engineering stared out from their completely un-heated rooms at icicles and snow on the window panes.

But the spring and autumn in east China are enchanting, much sung by the poets and writers of old: the fine scenery, lush vegetation, and soft living in this area south of the river appeared romantic and relaxed from the north.

It was to this part of the country that the weaker dynasties of China used to repair in past centuries when pressed by the rough-riding Tartar hordes from the north. The poets wrote of 'easy ladies of commercial talent, who knew not the bit-terness of alien rule and who still sang their tunes of "flowers in the back courtyards" when the enemy mounts were lining up to cross from the northern bank!' Life can be pleasant when it is not immediately threatened; one can have fun on the houseboats moored in canals or along the banks of a slow-flowing stream; the food can be delicate and delicious and the wine sweet. In describing this area south of the river in the spring, a famous line from a well-known poem, simply states: 'In the spring month of the third moon, the grass and weeds are long!' Indeed, with light mist shrouding the countryside in the mornings, and occasional warm drizzle falling in the afternoons, interspersed with shafts of warm sunshine which break through to brighten long periods of the day, the spring is a time of slow, lazy re-awakening – of lying in bed listening to the twittering birds at dawn and thinking of the flowers and petals which have fallen during the rain in the night, and not wanting to get up at all! This is the one region of China where spring is really memorable, even more than the brilliant autumn which anticipates the cold north wind.

However, my most vivid personal memories of the region are set in summer and autumn: racing down to the new Civic Centre in the brilliant sunshine of an October morning to attend the opening of the New Stadium in Shanghai, which was able to seat 100,000 people, and witness the commencement ceremonies of the National Olympics.

Around the stadium were clusters of food vendors and a built-in modern café where we used to eat, although the standard of food was undistinguished. But in down-town Shanghai you could eat the food of all nations as well as excellent local dishes; I shall never forget the mushroom soup at the Hsing Ya restaurant where my mother and my aunts often met for lunch, or the cooked knuckle of pork at the Ta Cha Li restaurant in Peking Road, or the snacks at Wu Yi Fang.

Spring in Shanghai

Wangpoo Crab Soup
Fu-Yung Diced Chicken
Meat Pudding with Red Bean-Curd Cheese

Pleasure Boat Duck
Red-cooked Lamb
Simmered Trout with Salted Cabbage
Vegetable Rice

WANGPOO CRAB SOUP

This soup is normally made from the miniature crabs which
thrive in Woosung, where the Wangpoo flows into the
mouth of the Yangtse, but it can, of course, also be prepared
from other crabs.

2–3 small crabs (about 1 lb.) or frozen or tinned crab in pieces
2 slices root ginger
1 medium onion (chopped)
½ pint chicken broth
1 teaspoon salt
3 tablespoons dry sherry
½ teaspoon M.S.G. (or chicken stock cube)
1½ tablespoons cornflour
½ pint of milk
1 tablespoon chopped ham
2 teaspoons lard

If using whole crabs, clean them thoroughly. Chop each
into four and boil gently with the ginger and onion in one
pint of water for twenty minutes. Skim off impurities and
filter the cooking liquid into the chicken broth through a fine
sieve or cheese cloth. With tinned or frozen crab, simmer
ginger and onion in 1 cup of water till it has reduced by half.
Add this flavoured water with the crab meat to the chicken
broth. Add salt and sherry. Bring to a gentle boil, skim off
any impurities. Add M.S.G. and cornflour blended with the
milk. Stir well until the soup thickens. Sprinkle with chopped
ham and lard (which adds richness), and serve in a tureen.

FU-YUNG DICED CHICKEN

6 oz. chicken breast
5 egg whites
2 teaspoons cornflour
1 teaspoon salt
4 tablespoons chicken broth
2 tablespoons chopped heart of spring greens (parboiled)
2 tablespoons vegetable oil
1 tablespoon chopped onion
1 teaspoon sugar
2 teaspoons light soya sauce

Chop chicken into ¼ in. cubes. Beat 1 egg white, the cornflour and half the salt together in a bowl for 15 seconds. Add the cubed chicken and mix well together.

Add half the chicken broth and the rest of salt to the remaining egg whites. Whisk together for ½ minute. Pour the mixture into a heatproof serving dish. Place the dish in a steamer and steam vigorously for 5–6 minutes. Sprinkle with chopped greens.

Meanwhile heat oil in a frying-pan. Add onion. Stir-fry over moderate heat for ½ minute. Add the remaining broth, the sugar and the soya sauce. Stir together, then add the cubed chicken. Continue to stir-fry gently for ½ minute.

Pour the chicken into the centre of the egg white in the serving dish, and serve.

MEAT PUDDING WITH RED BEAN CURD CHEESE

2½ lb. belly pork
2½ tablespoons red bean curd cheese (also called 'Southern Bean Curd Cheese')
1 large red pimento (sliced)
2 slices root ginger
1 medium onion (sliced)
2 teaspoons sugar
1 teaspoon salt
3 tablespoons dry sherry

Boil pork in a pan of water for 15 minutes. Remove and drain. Score the skin with a sharp knife ⅛ in. deep at 1 in. intervals to make 1 in. squares over the whole surface of the skin.

Now place the pork in a large casserole, add 1½ pints water and all the other ingredients. Cover tightly and place the casserole in a pre-heated oven at 375°F, gas 5, for 45 minutes. Reduce the temperature to 350°F, gas 4, and cook for another 45 minutes.

Now transfer the contents to a heatproof bowl. Place the pork in the bowl, skin side down. Pour the rest of the ingredients and liquid over the pork. Adjust seasoning and liquid (adding 2–3 tablespoons extra sherry, if desired), and place the bowl in a steamer for a further 40 minutes. Remove from steamer. Turn the pork on to a deep dish and serve skin side up together with sauce ingredients. The pork should now be so tender that it can be taken to pieces with a pair of chopsticks and shared according to the squares cut in the skin.

PLEASURE BOAT DUCK

Reputed to be called after the pleasure boats on Lake Taihu where the boatmen originated this style of cooking.

1 duck (2–3 lb.)
2 tablespoons vegetable oil
3 oz. lean pork
2 oz. broad beans
4 spring onions (cut in 2 in. segments)
3 oz. pickled salted cabbage
1 pint high broth (see p. 90 diluted with ½ pint water to make 1½ pints liquid)
6 tablespoons soya sauce
3 tablespoons dry sherry
2 slices root ginger

3 teaspoons sugar
½ teaspoon M.S.G. (or ½ chicken stock cube)
2 teaspoons cornflour (blended with 1 tablespoon water)
½ teaspoon sesame oil

Clean duck and remove head and feet. Dip it in a pan of boiling water for 2 minutes and drain.

Slice the pork and cabbage into strips. Heat 2 tablespoons oil in a frying-pan. Add onion, pork, cabbage and beans. Fry for 2 minutes. Add 6 tablespoons of broth and cook for 5 minutes. Stuff the duck with this mixture and sew up securely.

Paint the duck all over with soya sauce. Place it on a roasting pan and put it in an oven pre-heated to 400°F, gas 6, for 10 minutes. Paint and cook twice more until the duck has been roasted for 30 minutes in all.

Now place the duck in a heavy pan. Add remaining broth, sherry, sugar, ginger and remaining soya sauce. Bring the contents to the boil, then lower the heat and simmer for 1½ hours.

Transfer the duck to a large heatproof bowl. Pour the liquid left in the pan over the duck. Place the bowl in a steamer and steam for half an hour.

Remove the duck and place it in the centre of a serving dish. Heat the liquid remaining in the bowl in a small pan. Add the M.S.G., sesame oil, and cornflour; stir until the sauce thickens, pour it over the duck and serve.

RED-COOKED LAMB

2 lb. lamb (preferably leg)
¾ pint high broth (p. 90) diluted with ¾ pint water to give 1½ pints liquid
2 tablespoons dark soya sauce
4 tablespoons dry sherry
2 teaspoons sugar

1 tablespoon light soya sauce
1 medium onion (sliced)
½ teaspoon M.S.G. (or ½ chicken stock cube)
1 tablespoon chopped chives
½ teaspoon sesame oil

in a muslin bag

2 slices root ginger
1 tablespoon dried tangerine peel
2 cloves garlic
1 bouquet garni (parsley, thyme, bayleaf)

Wash lamb thoroughly, and stand in a basin of water for 2 hours. Wash again and drain.

Place the lamb in a heavy pan, add the broth and the muslin bag full of ingredients. Bring to the boil and cook for 10 minutes. Skim off scum. Add dark soya sauce, half the sherry and half the sugar. Simmer gently for 1 hour.

Transfer the lamb and all the liquid in the pan to a casserole. Add the remaining sherry, the remaining sugar, the light soya sauce, sliced onion and M.S.G. Cover and place the casserole in a pre-heated oven at 350°F, gas 4, and cook for a further 45 minutes. Remove the casserole from the oven, sprinkle contents with chopped chives and sesame oil and serve in the casserole.

SIMMERED TROUT WITH SALTED CABBAGE

4 trout (approximately 3 lb.)
3 tablespoons vegetable oil (or lard)
1 medium onion (chopped)
2 slices root ginger (chopped)
1 breakfast cup high broth (p. 90)
1 oz. salted cabbage (chopped)
1 oz. bamboo-shoots (cut into matchstick strips)
½ teaspoon salt
1 teaspoon sugar
2 tablespoons dry sherry
½ teaspoon M.S.G.

Clean the fish thoroughly and rinse under running water.
Heat oil in a frying-pan. Add onion and ginger and stir-fry
together over moderate heat for half a minute. Lay the fish
alongside one another in the oil and cook for 1 minute. Turn
them over and fry on the other side for 1 minute more. Pour
in the broth. Sprinkle the fish evenly with cabbage, bamboo-
shoots, salt, sugar, sherry and M.S.G. Cover the pan and
simmer for about 10 minutes, basting the fish with sauce now
and then. Serve in a deep dish, with the sauce poured over.

VEGETABLE RICE

Quite often in the spring in Shanghai, instead of plain boiled
rice, vegetable rice is served.

1 lb. long grain rice
½ lb. spring green hearts
2 tablespoons lard
½ teaspoon salt
1¼ pints water

Soak rice in water for 1 hour and drain. Chop the greens
into 2 in. pieces.

Heat lard in a large saucepan. When hot, add the greens
and stir-fry gently over moderate heat for 3 minutes. Add salt
and water. Stir until contents start to boil. Pour in the rice
and stir until contents boil again. Now turn down the heat to
its lowest and continue to stir gently clockwise so that the
rice and liquid move slowly around the pan (this prevents
sticking or burning). When the contents start to thicken, put
an asbestos sheet under the pan, and cover tightly. Continue
to simmer very gently for 10 minutes. Turn off the heat, but
allow the rice to stand in its own heat, still tightly covered,
for another 8 minutes. The contrast in colour between the
greens and the white rice is very attractive.

Summer in Shanghai

Peacock Hors d'Oeuvre
White Cut Pork
Drumsticks in Many-flavoured Sauce
Ham with Honey Syrup
Fried Spare Ribs with Pepper and Salt and Sweet and Sour
    Dips
Stir-fried Quick-braised 'Double Winter'
Date Paste Pancakes

PEACOCK HORS D'OEUVRES

3 hard-boiled eggs
3 oz. duck liver
1½ pints soya and herb sauce (see p. 153)
3 oz. duck meat
3 tablespoons vegetable oil
3 oz. chicken breast
3 oz. bamboo-shoots
2 stalks celery
½ teaspoon salt
½ teaspoon M.S.G.
6 tablespoons chicken broth
1 tablespoon soya sauce
1 tablespoon dry sherry
12 small dried Chinese mushrooms (soaked in warm water for 20
    minutes and stems removed)
2 oz. smoked ham
2 preserved 1,000-year-old eggs

The idea of this hors d'oeuvre is to interweave all the
different coloured ingredients, which are cut in thin slices or
in rounds in concentric circles resembling the pattern of a
peacock's feather.

Peel the boiled eggs and simmer them together with the
duck liver in the soya and herb sauce for 10 minutes. Add the

duck meat and simmer for another 10 minutes until they are quite brown. Drain. When cool cut into thin neat slices.

Heat 2 tablespoons oil in frying-pan, turn the chicken, bamboo-shoots and celery in it separately for 1 minute; then put them all in the pan. Sprinkle with salt and M.S.G. Add half the chicken broth. Turn the contents of the pan and simmer until nearly all the liquid has evaporated. Remove from pan. When cool slice into thin neat slices.

Heat the remaining tablespoon of oil, soya sauce, the remaining chicken broth, and sherry in a small frying-pan. Add the mushrooms, turning them over in the sauce. Heat gently for 3–4 minutes until nearly dry.

Cut the ham into neat 2 in. × ¾ in. pieces. Remove the shells and slice the preserved eggs into slices ¼ in. thick.

Arrange all the ingredients in concentric rings in contrasting colours on a very large round dish, or silver platter, and serve as an hors d'oeuvre to a party meal.

WHITE CUT PORK

3 lb. leg of pork
bottled shrimp sauce (for dipping)
high quality soya sauce (for dipping)

Place the pork in a pan of boiling water, and boil for 5 minutes. Pour away the water.

Place the pork in a heatproof dish. Invert another deep heatproof dish over it to cover and weight it down. Place the dishes with the pork in a large saucepan. Cover with water and bring to boil. Lower the heat and simmer gently for 1 hour.

Remove and drain the pork and allow it to cool naturally. When cold, cut into slices about 2 ins. × 1 in. × ¼ in. Arrange neatly in fish-scale fashion on a plate. Serve with shrimp sauce or a high-quality soya sauce dip. The dips should be placed conveniently around the table in small dishes.

DRUMSTICKS IN MANY-FLAVOURED SAUCE

10 chicken drumsticks
2 slices root ginger
2 spring onions (cut in 2 in. segments)
1 teaspoon salt
2 tablespoons lard
3 tablespoons chopped onion
1½ teaspoons curry powder
2 teaspoons sugar
¼ teaspoon five-spice powder
1 tablespoon light soya sauce
1½ teaspoons chilli sauce
2 tablespoons tomato purée
6 tablespoons chicken broth
½ chicken stock cube
3 teaspoons cornflour (blended in 2 tablespoons water)

Put the drumsticks in a pan of boiling water and boil for 2 minutes. Remove, drain, and transfer the drumsticks to a heatproof dish. Add the ginger and segments of spring onion and sprinkle with half the salt. Place in a steamer and steam for 45 minutes.

Heat lard in a frying-pan. When hot, add chopped onion and stir-fry over moderate heat for 1½ minutes. Add the remaining salt and the curry powder and stir-fry together for 1 minute. Add sugar and five-spice powder, stir and pour in the soya sauce, chilli sauce, tomato purée and chicken broth. Stir for 1½ minutes. Finally add chicken stock cube dissolved in a little hot water and cornflour. Stir until sauce thickens. When the drumsticks are done, discard the spring onion and ginger and place the drumsticks on a hot serving dish. Pour the sauce over and serve.

HAM WITH HONEY SYRUP

2 lb. York ham
3 tablespoons brown sugar
¼ teaspoon cinnamon
3 oz. lotus seeds (or raw unsalted peanuts parboiled for 15 minutes and chopped)
3 tablespoons honey
2 tablespoons white sugar
2 teaspoons cornflour (blended in 2 tablespoons water)

Steam the ham in a heatproof bowl for 1 hour. Remove, drain, and cool. Cut neatly in 1¼ in. squares about ⅓ in. thick. Arrange them on a round or oblong heatproof dish.

Heat brown sugar and cinnamon in 4 tablespoons water in a small saucepan. When the sugar has melted, add the lotus seeds and turn them in the syrup a few times. Using a spoon make a small pyramid of lotus seeds on top of each piece of ham.

Place the dish with the ham in a steamer and steam for 45 minutes.

Meanwhile heat honey and white sugar in 4 tablespoons water in a small pan. When the sugar has melted, add the blended cornflour. Stir, and when sauce thickens, pour a spoonful over each pile of lotus seeds on top of each piece of ham. Serve in the same dish.

FRIED SPARE RIBS WITH PEPPER AND SALT AND SWEET AND SOUR DIPS

The spare ribs are plain-fried, but are served and eaten with the two specially prepared dips.

2½ lb. meaty spare ribs

for salt and pepper mix
1½ tablespoons table salt
1 teaspoon black pepper

for the sweet and sour sauce

1½ tablespoons soya sauce
1½ tablespoons sugar
1½ tablespoons vinegar
1 tablespoon dry sherry
¾ tablespoon cornflour (blended in 4 tablespoons water)
1 tablespoon tomato purée
vegetable oil for deep frying

Mix all the ingredients for the sauce to a smooth consistency in a bowl. Heat the mixture gently in a small saucepan until it thickens. Pour into 2 small bowls.

Mix salt and pepper together, and spread on a small, dry frying-pan. Heat over low heat for 1½ minutes. Stir gently until you can smell a strong bouquet of pepper. Divide between two small dishes.

Clean the spare ribs and trim away any skin or gristle. Chop into 2 in. lengths. Heat oil in the deep-fryer. When very hot, lower the ribs into the oil in a wire basket and fry for ½ minute. Remove and drain over the pan for 1 minute. Deep-fry the ribs for another ½ minute. Drain and repeat a third time, by which time the ribs will be well cooked. Drain thoroughly and serve on a hot dish, accompanied by the sweet and sour sauce and the salt and pepper mix.

STIR-FRIED, QUICK-BRAISED DOUBLE WINTER

To serve winter products in the summer is typical of Chinese perversity.

10 medium dried Chinese winter mushrooms (soaked in warm water
    for 30 minutes and stalks removed)
5 oz. winter bamboo-shoots
2 tablespoons vegetable oil
2 tablespoons soya sauce
1½ teaspoons sugar

6 tablespoons chicken broth
½ teaspoon M.S.G.
2 teaspoons cornflour (blended in 2 tablespoons water)
1 teaspoon sesame oil

Quarter the mushrooms and cut the bamboo shoots into wedge-shaped pieces ½ in. thick.

Heat oil in a frying-pan. When very hot, lower the heat and add the bamboo-shoots. Stir-fry for ½ minute, add soya sauce and sugar. After stirring and tossing for 2 or 3 minutes add the mushrooms and chicken broth. Stir gently and cook together for 3 minutes. Add M.S.G. and cornflour mixture. When the sauce has thickened sprinkle with sesame oil and serve.

This dish is simple to cook and delicate in flavour and texture.

DATE PASTE PANCAKES

1½ lb. dates
½ lb. sugar
½ lb. flour
4 eggs
1½ breakfast cups milk
¼ pint vegetable oil
3 tablespoons sesame oil

Put the dates in a large heatproof bowl, place in a steamer and steam for 2½ hours. When cool, remove the stones and skin, and blend the fruit in a blender at high speed. Heat the sesame oil in a heavy saucepan, and add the date paste and sugar. Stir continuously over a low heat for 5 minutes and put aside.

Combine egg, flour and milk to make a runny batter.

Pour oil into a large, smooth frying-pan, swill it around and pour off surplus; place it over low heat and when the oil is hot pour in about ⅒th of the batter. Tilt the pan so that the

batter covers the surface of the pan evenly. Make pancake in
the normal way. Spread a thick layer of date paste down the
middle. Fold in both sides and turn the pancake over and fry
the other side for a few seconds. Lift the pancakes out onto
a warm plate. Slice fairly thinly and serve.

Autumn on the Lower Yangtze

Carp in Mutton Broth
Delicious-flavoured Duck Liver
Prawn Pouches
Chopped Pork Quick-fried with Bean Curd
Spring Bamboo-shoots in White Sauce
Red-cooked Duck, Soochow Style
Shredded Pears Garnished with Chopped Dates and Crys-
tallized fruit

CARP IN MUTTON BROTH

1½ lb. mutton
2 slices root ginger
1 clove garlic
1 onion (sliced)
1 teaspoon salt
1 lb. filleted carp
3 tablespoons dry sherry
½ teaspoon M.S.G.
1 tablespoon chopped chives

Cut mutton into 1½ in. cubes. Drop into a pan of boiling
water for 5 minutes. Pour away water. Add 3 pints fresh
water, onion, garlic, ginger and salt. Simmer gently for 2
hours.

Slice fish into 1½ in. squares. Place in a wire basket and
simmer them in a pan of boiling water for 2 minutes. Drain

and add them to the mutton and broth together with the sherry, M.S.G. and chives. Stir and simmer for 1 minute, then transfer the contents to a large heatproof bowl. Place the bowl in a steamer, steam vigorously for 10 minutes, and serve.

DELICIOUS-FLAVOURED DUCK LIVER

10 oz. duck liver
3 oz. chicken breast
1½ tablespoons cornflour (blended with 3 tablespoons water)
1 egg white
1 oz. bamboo-shoots
4 tablespoons duck fat
4 large dried Chinese mushrooms (soaked, stems removed and quartered)
3 tablespoons chicken broth
2 tablespoons dry sherry
¼ teaspoon salt
2 teaspoons light soya sauce
½ teaspoon M.S.G.
½ teaspoon sesame oil

Dip the livers in boiling water for 30 seconds. Drain and soak in a basin of fresh water for 15 minutes. Using a sharp knife, cut out the tubes and stringy bits and slice each liver into 2 flat slices. Cut chicken into similar flat slices.

Mix half the blended cornflour with egg white and beat together for 10 seconds. Add chicken and liver and mix them well together in a basin. Slice the bamboo-shoots like the chicken and liver.

Heat duck fat in a frying-pan until very hot. Add the liver, chicken, mushroom and bamboo-shoots and stir-fry for 2½ minutes. Remove, drain off fat and keep hot.

Now to the same pan add the chicken broth, sherry, salt, soya sauce, M.S.G. and remaining cornflour. Stir until the sauce thickens. Return the liver, chicken, mushrooms and

bamboo-shoots to the pan. Stir and turn until the pieces are
coated with the sauce. Add sesame oil. Give the contents one
more stir, and dish out onto a hot serving-dish.

PRAWN POUCHES

4 oz. prawns (shelled)
½ teaspoon salt
2 tablespoons dry sherry
2 teaspoons chopped chives (or spring onion)
4–6 tablespoons duck fat
6 eggs
4 tablespoons chicken broth
½ teaspoon M.S.G.
2 teaspoons light soya sauce
2 teaspoons cornflour (blended with 2 tablespoons water)

Chop each prawn into four. Place in a basin, add salt, chives,
half the sherry and 2 teaspoons duck fat and mix well.

Beat the eggs in a bowl for 10 seconds. Heat 3 tablespoons
duck fat in a small frying-pan over a low heat. When the fat
is quite hot, pour a dessertspoon of beaten egg in the centre of
the pan. Tip the pan so that the egg spreads out into a round
omelette. Before the centre of the egg has hardened, place a
level dessertspoon of prawns lightly on it. Using a slice or a
pair of chopsticks, fold one edge of the omelette over the
other. Baste with a spoonful of hot fat. Remove immediately
with a slice, and place it on a heatproof dish. Repeat, adding
more fat when necessary, until either the egg or prawns are
used up. Put the pouches in rows on the dish as they are
ready. Place the dish in a steamer and steam vigorously for 12
minutes.

Add chicken broth, soya sauce, M.S.G., cornflour and the
remaining sherry to the frying-pan (the fat in it will now be
nearly used up). Stir until it forms a thick sauce. Pour the
sauce over the egg-prawn pouches when they are taken out of
the steamer and serve.

CHOPPED PORK QUICK-FRIED WITH BEAN CURD

2 cakes bean curd (soaked in water for 10 minutes)
2 tablespoons lard
1 tablespoon chopped onion
3 teaspoons salted black beans (soaked in water for 20 minutes)
3 oz. lean pork (chopped very finely, but not minced)
2 oz. potato (peeled and chopped finely)
4 Chinese dried mushrooms (soaked in water for 20 minutes, stalks removed and quartered)
4 tablespoons high broth (see p. 90)
2 tablespoons dry sherry
1 teaspoon chilli sauce

Cut each bean curd cake into 6 pieces.

Heat lard in a frying-pan over moderate heat. Add onion and black beans and stir-fry for 1 minute. Add pork, potato, and mushrooms. Continue to stir-fry for 2 minutes. Add broth, sherry and chilli sauce. After stir-frying together gently for 10 seconds, put in the pieces of bean curd. Toss gently together and transfer to a heatproof serving dish. Place the dish in a steamer, steam vigorously for 10 minutes and serve.

SPRING BAMBOO-SHOOTS IN WHITE SAUCE

10 oz. tin bamboo-shoots
vegetable oil for deep-frying
6 tablespoons chicken broth
¼ teaspoon salt
½ teaspoon M.S.G.
1 tablespooon cornflour (blended in 2 tablespoons water)
4 tablespoons top of the milk
1 tablespoon chopped ham

Cut each bamboo-shoot in half. Give each piece a blow with the side of the kitchen chopper. Heat oil in a deep-fryer. When quite hot, place the bamboo-shoots in a wire basket and fry them in the hot oil for 3 minutes. Drain and arrange on a serving dish.

Heat broth, salt, M.S.G., top of the milk, and cornflour in a small pan, stirring constantly. When sauce thickens pour it over the bamboo-shoots. Garnish with the chopped ham and serve.

RED-COOKED DUCK, SOOCHOW STYLE

1 duck (3–4 lb.)
1 teaspoon salt
6 tablespoons soya sauce
3 tablespoons dry sherry
½ teaspoon cochineal (or red food-colouring)
¾ tablespoon cornflour (blended in 2 tablespoons water)

in a muslin bag

2 tablespoons dried tangerine peel
2 slices root ginger
4 tablespoons chopped onion
1 anise star
1 bouquet garni (parsley, thyme, bayleaf)

Place the duck in 2 pints water in a heavy saucepan. Bring to the boil and boil vigorously for 5 minutes. Skim off all scum. Add the herbs and onion in the muslin bag, and then salt, soya sauce, sherry, and colouring. Bring the contents to the boil again, then lower the heat and simmer for 1 hour. Turn the duck over and simmer over very low heat for another half hour.

Remove duck from the pan. Chop through the bone into 16–20 pieces and arrange on a serving dish.

Reserve two thirds of the gravy for other uses. Adjust the seasoning in the remaining gravy (adding a little more soya sauce or sherry, if desired), and add the cornflour. Stir over moderate heat until the gravy thickens. Pour this sauce over the duck and serve hot or cold.

SHREDDED PEARS GARNISHED WITH CHOPPED DATES
AND CRYSTALLIZED FRUITS

5 large pears
4 tablespoons ordinary or crystal sugar
8 tablespoons water
3 teaspoons cornflour (blended in 2 tablespoons water)
2 tablespoons chopped dates
2 tablespoons chopped crystallized cherries
2 tablespoons other colourful crystallized fruit, chopped

Peel the pears neatly. Remove stems and pips and slice into
matchstick strips. Arrange on a flat serving dish.

Heat sugar with water in a small pan. When sugar has all
melted add cornflour to thicken the syrup. Add the dates,
cherries and crystallized fruits. Mix together in the pan for 5
seconds. Spoon the fruits onto the pears and pour over the
syrup. Serve hot or chilled, with a dash of liqueur.

Winter on the Lower Yangtze

West Lake Watercress Soup
Chicken Marinated in Wine Sediment Paste
Lotus Leaf-wrapped Pork in Ground Rice
Fish Balls in Clear Soup
Shrimps in Tomato Sauce with Crackling Rice
Duck Casserole Flavoured with Onion and Tangerine
Date and Bean Paste Cakes

WEST LAKE WATERCRESS SOUP

¼ lb. watercress
2 oz. chicken breast
4 oz. ham
2 teaspoons cornflour
1½ pints high broth (see p. 90)
1 teaspoon salt
1 teaspoon chicken fat

Clean watercress thoroughly, cutting away the muddier
white roots. Simmer the ham in the high broth for 20
minutes. Remove the ham, cut 3 oz. of it into fine strips and
return it to the broth. Shred the last ounce and reserve for
garnish. Cut chicken into matchstick-sized strips, sprinkle
with cornflour and rub it in thoroughly.

Dip watercress in a pan of boiling water for 10 seconds,
remove and drain, and place at the bottom of the soup
tureen.

Heat broth in a saucepan. Add salt, drop in the chicken
and simmer for 1 minute. Pour the broth and other ingredients over the watercress in the soup bowl. Add chicken fat
to the soup, sprinkle with 1 oz. shredded ham and serve.

CHICKEN MARINATED IN WINE SEDIMENT PASTE

1 capon (4–5 lb.)
3 teaspoons salt
3 slices root ginger (chopped)
½ pint wine sediment paste (see p. 165)
1 breakfast cup dry sherry

After cleaning the bird thoroughly, rub it inside and out with
1½ teaspoons salt. Steam the bird for 1 hour. Leave to cool and
chop it in half through the bone.

Mix wine sediment paste and sherry in a pan. Add remaining salt and ginger and steam this mixture for 20 minutes.

Pour one third of the mixture into an earthenware casserole, spreading it out evenly, and cover with a piece of
cloth. Lay the two halves of the capon in the centre of the
cloth. Lay another piece of cloth over the capon. Pour the
remaining wine sediment paste mixture evenly over the
cloth. Cover the casserole tightly and leave it to stand for 1
week. Remove the top cloth from the bird, chop it into 16–20
pieces and serve.

LOTUS LEAF-WRAPPED PORK IN GROUND RICE

2 lb. belly pork (without skin)

for the marinade

½ teaspoon salt
1½ tablespoons hoisin sauce
1 tablespoon soya sauce
1 tablespoon sherry
1 tablespoon chopped onion
2 slices root ginger (chopped)

3 oz. rice
1 tablespoon dried tangerine peel
¼ teaspoon five-spice powder
1 sheet lotus leaf
6 long spring onions

Cut pork into 6 equal-sized oblong pieces. Mix, salt, hoisin sauce, soya sauce, sherry, chopped onion and ginger in a basin. Add the pork and marinate for 2 hours.

Heat rice and tangerine peel in a dry pan over low heat until rice just turns yellow. Grind the two together coarsely, add the five-spice powder and mix well.

Remove the pork from the marinade, drain, and coat the pieces evenly with the ground rice mixture.

Soak lotus leaf in hot water. When it has softened cut into six pieces suitable for wrapping the pork. Wrap each piece of pork in a piece of lotus leaf; tie securely with a stalk of spring onion. Place all the parcels on a heatproof dish and steam for 2½ hours. Bring the dish to the table and let each person serve himself a parcel.

FISH BALLS IN CLEAR SOUP

2 lb. filleted fish (halibut, haddock, cod)
2 tablespoons onion (finely chopped)
2 tablespoons smoked ham (finely chopped)

2 slices root ginger (finely chopped)
¾ teaspoon salt
1 tablespoon dry sherry

for the soup

¾ pint chicken broth
½ teaspoon salt
½ teaspoon M.S.G. (or chicken stock cube)
1 oz. bamboo-shoots (sliced)
4 large dried mushrooms (soaked for 20 minutes, quartered and stalks removed)
1 spring onion cut in 1 in. segments
2 teaspoons lard

First slice the fish. Place the slices in water to soak for half an hour. Drain and chop finely on a chopping block (but do not mince).

Now place the fish in a bowl with 4 tablespoons water and ¼ teaspoon salt. Beat with a fork or pair of chopsticks for at least 5–6 minutes or blend in an electric blender until there are small bubbles in the fish mixture. Add another 3 tablespoons water and ½ teaspoon salt, and blend or beat again for at least 5–6 minutes more. By this time the fish mixture will be ready to be made into balls. Test by placing a small quantity of the fish in water; if it floats it is ready. If not beat or blend a little longer.

When the fish paste is ready, add the chopped onion, ham, ginger and sherry and mix together. Now form fish balls about the size of a chestnut by squeezing a handful of mixture through the hole made by the index finger and the thumb. Put all the fish balls on a large plate in the refrigerator for half an hour, to chill and firm up.

Now drop the fish balls gently into a large pan of nearly boiling water (keep the water just off the boil as otherwise the fish balls will harden; they should be soft and springy). Move the balls around gently in the water for 6–7 minutes until they have turned quite white. Remove, drain, and place them in a deep dish.

To prepare the soup, bring the chicken broth to the boil, add salt, M.S.G., bamboo-shoots, mushrooms and onions and simmer for 5 minutes. Finally add the lard. When that has melted pour the soup over the fish balls and serve. This should be treated as a savoury dish rather than as a soup.

SHRIMPS IN TOMATO SAUCE WITH CRACKLING RICE

½ lb. shrimps
¼ teaspoon salt
1 tablespoon dry sherry
1 tablespoon cornflour
2 tablespoons lard
3 oz. pot-stuck rice (scraped off the bottom of rice cooker)
oil for deep-frying

for tomato sauce:

6 tablespoons chicken broth
¼ teaspoon salt
¼ teaspoon M.S.G.
3 tablespoons tomato purée
1 tablespoon dry sherry
¾ tablespoon cornflour (blended in 1½ tablespoons water)

Heat pot-stuck rice in oven until very dry. Add salt and sherry to shrimps and sprinkle with cornflour. Mix well and allow them to stand for 1 hour.

Heat lard in a frying-pan. When it has melted, add the shrimps. Spread them out and stir-fry gently for 1 minute. Remove and keep warm.

Now add chicken broth and all the other ingredients for the sauce to the pan. Stir gently over moderate heat until the mixture thickens. Return the shrimps to the pan. Turn and mix together for ½ minute and place in a hot bowl.

Place the dried pot-stuck rice (or rice scrapings) in a fine wire basket. Heat the oil in the deep-fryer. When very hot, fry the rice in it for ¾ – 1 minute when it should start to turn brown.

Drain the crackling rice and place it quickly in a large, hot serving bowl. Pour the shrimps over the rice at the table. The rice crackles audibly, and this makes an unusual and colourful dish for a party.

DUCK CASSEROLE FLAVOURED WITH ONION AND TANGERINE

1 duck (3–4 lb.)
2 oz. sliced bamboo-shoots
4 large Chinese dried mushrooms (soaked, quartered and stems removed)
5 tablespoons soya sauce
3 tablespoons sherry
3 spring onions (cut in 2 in. segments)
peel of 1 fresh tangerine
3 tablespoons lard

Clean duck thoroughly and place in a pan of boiling water to simmer for 10 minutes. Remove duck and discard water. Place the duck in a casserole and add just sufficient water to cover it. Add bamboo-shoots, mushrooms and soya sauce. Place in the oven at 375°F, gas 5, for 1 hour. Turn the duck over, skim off any excess fat, add sherry and return the casserole to the oven to cook at 350°F, gas 4, for another hour.

Remove the casserole from the oven and skim off any excess fat.

Heat lard in a small frying-pan. When it has melted add the segments of onion and the pieces of tangerine peel. Stir-fry over moderate heat for 2 minutes. Strain the flavoured fat over the whole duck and serve. The duck should be sufficiently tender to be dismembered with a pair of chopsticks.

DATE AND BEAN PASTE CAKES

1 lb. red or ordinary dates
6 oz. sweetened bean paste (see p. 242)
1 lb. sugar
6 oz. ground rice
6 oz. ground glutinous rice
3 oz. lard
4 oz. suet

Simmer dates in 1½ pints of water for 40 minutes or until the skin and stones can be easily removed. Retain water and mash dates to a paste.

Place the paste in a large basin. Stir in the bean paste, sugar, lard, suet, ground rice and glutinous rice. Add the hot date water to the basin. Mix the contents together thoroughly with a wooden spoon until the mixture is smooth.

Grease a deep heatproof dish, and put in the mixture. Place the dish in a steamer and steam for 50 minutes. Turn the 'cake' out, and cut it into 1½ in. triangular-shaped pieces. Serve as a dessert, with cream if you like.

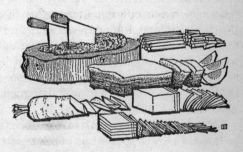

Seasons in West and West-Central China

Perhaps the coastal Chinese feel familiar with western China because The Story of the Three Kingdoms (the Chinese equivalent of King Arthur and the Knights of the Round Table) was set mainly in Szechuan. Actually, the majority only came to know it when they moved to the great interior during the Japanese War. It is one of the largest provinces and certainly the most heavily populated in the whole of China. Szechuan is a vast basin, bounded by ranges of mountains, and thus not afflicted by the monsoons of the coast, nor the freezing seasonal winds from the north.

Much of China is conducive to luxuriant vegetation, and the west is no exception; in summer this region is very humid, and vegetation runs riot in the near tropical heat. Although the winter is not severe, the houses are, in general, inadequately heated, and one can only keep warm by putting on layers of warm clothing until one is quite stiffly upholstered.

Further south-west is the province of Yunnan, which in Chinese means 'South of the Clouds'; the very name conjures up a feeling of distance. Unlike the American south-west, which is arid, this is the one region in China where the mountains and rivers run north-south, rather than east-west, and the climate is ideal. Kunming, one of the main towns, stands at an altitude of 5,000 feet, and is considered to have the best weather in the whole of China. Specks of high-flying white cloud move across the blue sky, and a dozen miles away is the Ear-Shaped Sea, a lake of some forty square miles, where a wide variety of fish abound.

But now, nearly thirty years later, when talking to friends and colleagues who spent years in this region during the war, hardly any of us can remember clearly the quality of the food we ate. We must all have been so starved that we simply ate everything that came our way; our sense of taste and delicacy of palate in this period were not to be trusted. Everything was grist to our mill.

So, to make a balanced assessment, I have re-examined the

recipes which originate from this region in order to remind myself of the considerable variety of foods for which the area is well known. Indeed, some of the dishes are famous and well established as far afield as the cities on the east coast, in fact, in every part of China and especially in Peking itself. Here is a selection.

Spring in Szechuan

Minced Chicken and Green Pea Soup
Crispy Barbecue of Rib and Belly Pork
Hot-fried Shredded Carp with Celery
Tangerine Peel Quick-fried Chicken in Hot Sauce
Double-cooked Pork
Hot Celery Cabbage
Fruit Salad in Almond Syrup

MINCED CHICKEN AND GREEN PEA SOUP

3 oz. chicken breast
2 egg whites (lightly beaten)
1 teaspoon salt
6 oz. peas
1 teaspoon chicken fat
½ teaspoon M.S.G.
2 tablespoon cornflour (blended in 4 tablespoons water)
1½ pints chicken broth

Mince the chicken, beat in egg whites, a third of the salt and half the cornflour. Heat ½ pint of the chicken broth in a small saucepan. Gradually stir in the chicken mixture, stirring all the time until the liquid thickens into a thick white soup. Put on a low fire to keep warm.

Cook the peas in boiling water for 20 minutes. Drain and put through a blender at high speed. Heat the remaining pint

of chicken broth in a large saucepan. Add the remaining salt,
M.S.G., and the purée. Stir in the second tablespoon of
cornflour to thicken, and sprinkle with chicken fat to enrich
the soup and make it smooth. It should have a good green
colour.

Put the pea soup into a large soup tureen and pour the
white chicken soup into the middle and serve as a two-toned
soup.

CRISPY BARBECUE OF RIB AND BELLY PORK

1 square piece rib-belly pork (belly with ribs attached; choose a meaty
    piece with minimal fat, weighing approx. 6–7 lb.)
1 egg white
2 tablespoons cornflour (blended to a paste with beaten egg white)

Best cooked under a large grill in a normal western kitchen.

Clean the pork, and use a skewer to poke half a dozen holes
through the skin in between each pair of ribs.

Place the pork under the grill, and grill for about 15
minutes at high heat, a little more than half the time with
skin towards the heat. To finish, grill the skin side for an
extra 3 to 4 minutes, until the skin is quite burnt.

Remove the pork from the grill, immerse it in warm water,
and scrape off the burnt skin. Drain and dry the pork with a
cloth. Coat the skin side with a light layer of cornflour paste.
Now place the pork under the grill and reduce the heat by
one third. Grill the rib side for 5–6 minutes, and the skin side
for 7–8 minutes.

Cut the skin from the ribs, and cut it again into 1 in.–2 in.
squares; serve on a warmed dish. Cut the meat on the bone
into individual ribs and serve on a separate dish.

The skin and meat should be eaten with flower rolls (see p.
233), and with various dips: plum sauce, chopped spring
onion in concentrated chicken broth (6 tablespoons broth
with ½ teaspoon M.S.G. added), and chopped garlic in soya

sauce (2 cloves chopped in 4 tablespoons soya sauce). The dips are placed on the dining table in saucers or small dishes.

HOT-FRIED SHREDDED CARP WITH CELERY

½ lb. filleted carp
1 egg white
1½ tablespoons cornflour
½ teaspoon salt
½ lb. celery heart
4 tablespoons lard
2 slices root ginger (chopped finely)
3 spring onions (cut in 2 in. lengths)
2 chilli peppers (chopped and seeded)
1 tablespoon light soya sauce
1½ teaspoons vinegar
1½ teaspoons sugar
3 tablespoons chicken broth
½ teaspoon M.S.G.
1 tablespoon sherry
1 teaspoon sesame oil

Cut the fish into matchstick-sized strips. Beat egg white, cornflour, and salt together into a runny paste. Pour it over the fish and mix evenly.

Shred celery into similar matchstick-sized pieces.

Heat lard in a frying-pan over moderate heat. When it has melted, add fish, spreading it evenly over the pan. Turn the fish over gently with a slice or perforated spoon. Remove pan from the fire, turn a few more times then remove the fish from the pan. Drain the fat back into the pan and keep hot.

Add the ginger, spring onions, and chillis and stir-fry for ½ minute over high heat. Add the shredded celery and continue to stir-fry for 1 minute. Add the soya sauce, vinegar, sugar, chicken broth, and M.S.G. Stir and toss for 1 minute. Return the fish to the pan and mix gently with the celery. Sprinkle with sherry and sesame oil. After turning and tossing once or twice more, serve on a warmed dish.

TANGERINE PEEL QUICK-FRIED CHICKEN IN HOT SAUCE

1 spring chicken (approx. 2 lb.)
1 onion (sliced)
3 slices root ginger
3 tablespoons dry sherry
1 teaspoon salt
2 chilli peppers (seeded and chopped)
1 tablespoon dried tangerine peel (or use 1 large fresh peel broken into small pieces)
2 teaspoons sugar
2 teaspoons wine vinegar
good pinch black pepper
3 tablespoons soya sauce
6 tablespoons vegetable oil
1 teaspoon seasame oil

Chop the chicken through the bone into 16–20 pieces (see pp. 121–2). Add ginger and onion, sprinkle with salt and 1 tablespoon each of soya sauce and sherry. Work this marinade into the chicken with fingers and leave to marinate for half an hour, then remove ginger and onion.

Heat oil in a large frying-pan. When hot add the marinated chicken. Turn and fry for 3½ minutes, then remove and drain and pour away any excess oil.

Add the chilli pepper and tangerine peel to the remaining oil in the pan. After 15 seconds stir-frying over high heat, return the chicken to the pan. Turn the chicken completely over once. Mix the rest of the sherry and soya sauce, the vinegar, sugar, and pepper in a bowl; pour evenly over the chicken. Stir-fry for a further ½ minute, sprinkle with sesame oil, and serve.

DOUBLE-COOKED PORK

2 lb. lean and fat pork
6 tablespoons vegetable oil

1 green sweet pepper (chopped and seeded)
1 dry chilli pepper (seeded and chopped)
3 teaspoons salted beans (soaked in water 20 minutes, drained and
  chopped)
1 slice root ginger (chopped)
2 tablespoons spring onion (chopped)
2 cloves garlic (chopped)
½ teaspoon salt
1 tablespoon hoisin sauce
1 tablespoon bean paste
2 teaspoons sugar
1 tablespoon soya sauce
3 tablespoons dry sherry

Boil the pork in water for 20 minutes. Drain, and slice into 2
in. × 1 in. × ⅛ in. pieces, through lean and fat.

Heat oil in a large frying-pan. When very hot, add the
pieces of pork, spread them out and fry over high heat for 2
minutes. Remove and drain, pouring any excess oil back into
the pan.

Add shredded green pepper, salted beans and chilli pepper
to the remaining oil. Stir-fry together for ½ minute. Add salt,
onion, ginger, garlic, hoisin sauce, and bean paste. Stir-fry
together for 15 seconds. Add sherry, soya sauce, and sugar.
After stirring a few times to mix together, return the pork
to the pan. Stir-fry for ½ minute and serve. This is a typical
Szechuan dish which is well known in the outer provinces.

HOT CELERY CABBAGE

1 lb. celery cabbage (if unavailable use Savoy cabbage or celery)
1 tablespoon salt
2 tablespoons vegetable oil
1 tablespoon shredded root ginger
1 tablespoon shredded chilli pepper (seeded)
2 tablespoons shredded sweet red pepper
1 tablespoon sesame oil
1½ tablespoons sugar

1½ tablespoons wine vinegar
1½ tablespoons light soya sauce
3 tablespoons chicken broth

Cut cabbage into pieces 2 ins. long. Soak in brine (1 tablespoon salt to 1 pint water) for 2 hours. Remove and drain.

Heat vegetable oil in a large frying-pan. Add ginger and
chilli pepper. Stir-fry together for ½ minute. Add the cabbage,
and turn it in the oil over high heat for 2½ minutes. Remove
and arrange on serving dish.

Now add sesame oil and red pepper to the frying-pan. Stir-
fry for 15 seconds over moderate heat. Pour in the soya sauce,
vinegar, broth, and sugar. Stir for 15 seconds. Pour the mixture over the cabbage as dressing and garnish.

This cabbage is hot, as well as sweet and sour.

FRUIT SALAD IN ALMOND SYRUP

3 peaches
3 apples
6 tablespoons lichees
6 tablespoons cherries
4 slices pineapple
3 tablespoons ground almonds
2 tablespoons ground glutinous rice
2 tablespoons cornflour (blended in 4 tablespoons water)
6 tablespoons sugar

Dice the apples, peaches and pineapple as a fruit salad. Add
the lichees and cherries and mix all the fruits together in a
large bowl.

Mix the almonds, rice and sugar in ¾ pint water. Heat to
near boiling. Simmer gently for 10 minutes stirring continuously. Add the cornflour to thicken further. Stir over low
heat for another 2–3 minutes. Pour the syrup over the fruit
salad; serve hot or well-chilled.

Szechuan in the Summer

Fish and Heart of Spring Greens Soup
Thin Sliced Quick-braised Beef
Sliced Sweet and Sour Pork on Crackling Rice
Pan-fried Bean Curd
Cold Shredded Venison
Quick-fried Hot Diced Chicken
Silver Tree-fungi in Crystal Syrup

FISH AND HEART OF SPRING GREENS SOUP

6 oz. filleted fish (carp, haddock, sole, halibut, mullet, bass)
1 cake bean curd
4 medium Chinese dried mushrooms (soaked and stems removed)
1 tablespoon chopped onion
2 teaspoons salted black beans (soaked for 10 minutes, drained and chopped)
2 pints high broth (see p. 90)
2 oz. chicken breast (sliced)
2 oz. smoked ham (sliced)
6 oz. spring greens (outer leaves discarded, hearts sliced vertically in four)
1 teaspoon salt
1 tablespoon light soya sauce
2 tablespoons sherry
1 tablespoon cornflour (blended in 2 tablespoons water)
½ teaspoon M.S.G. (or chicken stock cube)
oil for deep-frying

Cut fish into 1½ in. × 1 in. pieces, the bean curd into 10 pieces, and quarter each mushroom.

Heat oil in the deep-fryer. When very hot, lower in the pieces of fish in a wire basket and fry for 1 minute. Drain.

Heat 3 teaspoons oil in a large saucepan. Add onion and salted black beans. Stir-fry together for ½ minute, then add the high broth. When it starts to boil, reduce the heat, add chicken, ham, bean curd, greens, mushrooms, salt, soya sauce and sherry and simmer gently for 10 minutes. Add fish and simmer for a further 3 minutes. Add cornflour and M.S.G. Stir gently for 15 seconds. Pour the soup into a large tureen and serve.

THIN SLICED QUICK-BRAISED BEEF

1 lb. fillet of beef
2 tablespoons vegetable oil
2 tablespoons chopped onion
1 slice root ginger (chopped)
1 teaspoon salted beans (soaked for 10 minutes, drained and chopped)
4 asparagus stalks (cut diagonally into 1½ in. segments)
1 tablespoon hoisin sauce
½ pint high broth (p. 90)
2 tablespoons dry sherry
1 tablespoon light soya sauce
2 spring onions (cut in 1 in. segments)
½ teaspoon M.S.G.
1 tablespoon cornflour (blended with 6 tablespoons milk)

for the marinade
½ teaspoon salt
2 teaspoons light soya sauce
½ tablespoon cornflour

Slice beef with a sharp knife into razor-thin slices 2 ins. × 1 in. Sprinkle with the three marinade ingredients; mix together well and leave to marinate for 1 hour.

Heat oil in a deep frying-pan. When hot, add chopped onion, ginger, and salted beans. Stir-fry together for ½ minute over moderate heat. Add asparagus and hoisin sauce and stir-fry for another ½ minute. Pour in the broth, sherry and the tablespoon of sauce. Bring to boil and then simmer gently for 10 minutes.

Turn the heat up to its highest. Add the spring onions and beef. Use a pair of chopsticks or perforated spoon to spread the beef out evenly, mixing it with onion and asparagus.

After cooking for ½ minute at high heat, add the M.S.G. and cornflour in milk. Stir until the sauce thickens and serve immediately on a warmed, deep dish.

SLICED SWEET AND SOUR PORK ON CRACKLING RICE

3 oz. dried rice scrapings (from bottom of rice pan)
6 oz. lean pork
½ teaspoon salt
½ tablespoon cornflour
1 oz. bamboo-shoots (sliced)
1 green pimento (seeded and cut in slices)
1 small onion (chopped)
1 slice root ginger
1 clove garlic (chopped)
vegetable oil for deep-frying

for sauce

1 tablespoon soya sauce
1½ tablespoons vinegar
1½ tablespoons sugar
1½ tablespoons tomato sauce
4 tablespoons chicken broth
1 tablespoon cornflour

Break up the rice scrapings and place on a roasting pan to dry in an oven at 325°F, gas 3, for 15 minutes, then turn heat off.

Slice pork into thin slices 1 in. × 1 in. Rub salt and cornflour into the pork. Mix sauce ingredients in a bowl until smooth.

Heat 3 tablespoons oil in a frying-pan. When hot add the pork, spreading it out. Stir-fry for 4 minutes. Remove, drain and put aside.

Return frying-pan to the heat. Add bamboo-shoots, pimento, onion, ginger and garlic and stir-fry together over moderate heat for 1 minute. Pour in the sauce mixture. Stir until the sauce thickens and is translucent.

Now return the pork to the frying-pan. Mix thoroughly with the sauce so that each piece is well coated.

Meanwhile place the rice scrapings in a wire basket. Lower it into hot oil in the deep-fryer for 1½ minutes. Drain well and place immediately on a hot dish. Pour the pork and sauce over it at the table, which makes an entertaining crackling noise.

PAN-FRIED BEAN CURD

4 bean curd cakes (chopped)
2 egg whites
½ teaspoon salt
1 teaspoon flour
2 teaspoons cornflour
½ teaspoon M.S.G.
2 teaspoons lard
½ lb. belly pork (without skin)
1 tablespoon cornflour (blended with 1 beaten egg)
2 tablespoons smoked ham (minced)
5 oz. french beans
3 tablespoons vegetable oil

for dressing

3 teaspoons sugar
3 teaspoons vinegar
3 teaspoons sesame oil

Beat egg whites until quite stiff. Add salt, flour, 2 teaspoons cornflour, M.S.G., lard and finally, chopped bean curd. Mix them well together, and form this mixture into small squares.

Slice pork into a dozen thin, square slices across the lean and fat. Make a diagonal cut on the surface of each slice (to prevent it from curling up when fried).

Coat each slice of pork with the cornflour and beaten egg paste. Place a piece of bean curd mixture on top of each piece of pork and press firmly together. Sprinkle the top of each with a pinch of minced ham and place all these little squares in a heatproof dish in a steamer for 10 minutes, then remove.

Parboil french beans for 3 minutes, drain and stir-fry them in a small pan with 1 tablespoon oil for 2 minutes. Place them at one end of an oval dish. Whisk the ingredients for the dressing together for ½ minute and pour it over the beans.

Heat 2 tablespoons oil in a large frying-pan. Tilt the pan so that the whole base is covered with oil.

Arrange the pieces of pork and bean curd in the pan. Hold the pan above moderate heat, moving it gently all the time, so that the heat will spread evenly. Heat in this manner for 7–8 minutes. Place the pork and bean curd squares at the other end of the vegetable dish and serve. The dish satisfies the Chinese concern with contrasting colours, flavours, and food materials.

COLD SHREDDED VENISON

1½ lb. venison
2 medium onions (sliced)
3 slices root ginger (shredded)
4 tablespoons dry sherry
1½ tablespoons chopped chives

for dressing

2 teaspoons salad oil
1½ teaspoons sesame oil
1½ tablespoons soya sauce
½ teaspoon chilli oil
1 tablespoon sherry
good pinch black pepper
½ teaspoon M.S.G.
1 tablespoon chicken broth

Dip the venison in boiling water for 3 minutes and then drain. Clean thoroughly and place in a basin. Spread ginger and onion on top and sprinkle with sherry. Place the basin in a steamer to steam vigorously for 40 minutes.

Remove venison from basin and discard ginger and onion. Slice the meat first into slices, and cut again along the grain into matchstick-sized strips.

Arrange the shredded venison on a serving dish. Sprinkle with chopped chives. Beat the ingredients for the dressing together for 15 seconds, and pour over the venison. An excellent dish which is specially good with wine.

QUICK-FRIED HOT DICED CHICKEN

1 lb. chicken breast
½ teaspoon salt
1 egg white
1 tablespoon cornflour
1 sweet red pepper
2 tablespoons vegetable oil
2 tablespoons lard
2 dried chilli peppers (quartered and seeds removed)
1 tablespoon chopped onion
1 slice root ginger (chopped)
1 tablespoon light soya sauce
1 tablespoon dry sherry
2 teaspoons tomato purée
1 teaspoon wine vinegar
1 tablespoon chicken broth

Dice chicken into ⅓ in. cubes, and rub in salt. Beat egg white for 5 seconds and add cornflour to make a batter. Mix cubed chicken evenly with the batter.

Slice sweet pepper into pieces ½ in. square.

Heat 2 tablespoons oil in a frying-pan over moderate heat. Tilt the pan so the whole base is covered. Add the chicken, spreading it out quickly. Stir-fry for 2 minutes and remove.

Add lard to the pan, and then chilli peppers, onion, ginger and sweet pepper. Stir-fry for 1½ minutes. Add soya sauce, sherry, tomato purée, wine vinegar and chicken broth. Stir-fry together for ½ minute.

Return the chicken to the pan. Stir-fry together for another ½ minute. Turn out onto a dish and serve.

SILVER TREE-FUNGI IN CRYSTAL SOUP

1 oz. dried silver fungi (available from most Chinese food stores)
1 egg
½ lb. crystal sugar (in lumps)
1½ pints water

Soak fungi in warm water for 1½ hours. Clean thoroughly and place in a bowl of fresh water. Break the clusters into individual pieces.

Beat egg for 10 seconds, add 4 tablespoons water and beat together for 5 more seconds.

Heat sugar and water in a very clean enamel pan. When sugar has all melted, and it is just about to boil, pour in the beaten egg. Stir it around once in the pan. When the egg has coagulated into a cloud, pour the syrup in the pan through a fine sieve into a heatproof soup bowl (this process helps to clarify it). Ladle the fungi into the bowl with a perforated spoon. Place the bowl in a steamer and steam for 1½ hours. Serve in the bowl, warm or chilled.

Autumn in the South-West

Bamboo-shoot Soup
Cold-sliced Long-simmered Beef
Red-cooked Venison Heels
Wind-dried Sweet-cooked Pork from Kunming
Sliced Chicken with Walnuts
Yunnan Fish Casserole
Wu Family Sweet Dumpling Balls

BAMBOO-SHOOT SOUP

¾ lb. tender bamboo-shoots (or tinned or fresh asparagus tips)
3 oz. lean and fat pork
2 oz. smoked ham
2 teaspoons cornflour
3 oz. broccoli
1½ pints high broth (p. 90)
1 teaspoon salt
¼ teaspoon M.S.G. (or chicken stock cube)
2 tablespoons dry sherry
oil for deep-frying
1 teaspoon sesame oil

If using fresh asparagus tips parboil them for three minutes.
Cut bamboo-shoots diagonally into 1½ in. × ¼ in. × ¼ in.
strips. Slice pork into very thin slices 1 in. × ½ in., and rub in
the cornflour. Cut ham into similar slices. Cut broccoli into
pieces of about 1½ ins.

Heat broth in a saucepan. Add salt, pork, ham, and broccoli. Bring to boil and simmer gently for 10 minutes.

Deep-fry bamboo-shoots in hot oil for 2½ minutes. Drain
thoroughly, and add to the broth along with M.S.G. and
sherry. Simmer for 2 minutes, sprinkle with sesame oil and
serve in a large tureen.

COLD-SLICED LONG-SIMMERED BEEF

4 lb. shin of beef
1½ tablespoons salt
2 slices root ginger
1 bouquet garni

for table dips

plum sauce, hoisin sauce, salt and pepper mix (see p. 240),
sesame jam, chilli sauce, soya sauce (high quality)

Dissolve salt in 2 pints water and soak beef in it for 2
hours.

Rinse beef in fresh water, and place it in a pan of boiling water for 5 minutes. Discard water, and replace with fresh water. Bring to boil, add ginger, bouquet garni, and simmer gently (with an asbestos sheet underneath the pan) for 4 hours over the lowest heat, adding more water, when necessary, to keep the beef covered.

Remove beef from the pan, drain, and slice with a sharp knife into pieces 1½ ins. × 1 in. × ⅛ in. Arrange neatly on a dish and serve with the various dips.

RED-COOKED VENISON HEELS

1½ lb. venison heels (or calves' feet)
6 oz. chicken (sliced)
6 oz. ham (sliced)
1 tablespoon oyster sauce
½ teaspoon salt
2 tablespoons dry sherry
2 tablespoons lard
1 tablespoon chopped onion
2 slices root ginger
2 tablespoons salted cabbage
2 oz. celery cabbage (sliced; or celery, or Savoy cabbage)
2 oz. bamboo-shoots (sliced)
½ breakfast cup chicken broth
1½ teaspoons soya sauce
2 tablespoons coriander leaves (chopped)
1 teaspoon sesame oil

Simmer the venison heels gently in water for 3 hours, skimming the surface as necessary. Drain and cut away any skin or gristle. Rinse under fresh water, drain and put aside. Cut into 1½ in. × 1 in. segments.

Place the heels at the bottom of a heatproof bowl, place the pieces of chicken and ham on top, and sprinkle with oyster sauce, salt and sherry. Place the bowl in a steamer and steam vigorously for 1 hour.

Meanwhile, heat lard in a frying-pan. Add onion, ginger and salted cabbage. Stir-fry for 1 minute over high heat. Add celery cabbage and bamboo-shoots (thinly sliced). Stir-fry for 1 minute. Add broth and soya sauce. Simmer the contents over moderate heat for 5 minutes. Pour this mixture into the bowl containing the venison heels. Steam for a further 15 minutes. Turn the contents of the bowl out into a deep serving dish. Sprinkle the venison heels with coriander leaves and sesame oil and serve.

WIND-DRIED SWEET-COOKED PORK FROM KUNMING

2½ lb. leg of pork
4 tablespoons lard

for sauce

2 tablespoons sugar
1 tablespoon wine vinegar
1 tablespoon soya sauce
½ tablespoon bean paste
1 teaspoon chilli sauce
½ tablespoon hoisin sauce
2 teaspoons cornflour (blended in 2 tablespoons water)

Slice pork into pieces 2 ins. × 1½ ins. × ⅛ in. Spread out the slices in a colander in an airy spot to dry completely for 3 hours.

Mix sauce ingredients thoroughly. Heat lard in a large pan, spreading it so that it covers the whole of the base. Add the pork, spreading the pieces out, so that each piece is in contact with the pan, and fry over low heat without stirring for 5 minutes, turning the pieces over once. Remove pork and drain off any excess fat.

Pour the sauce mixture into the pan. Mix with the remaining fat for ½ minute over low heat. Return the pork to the pan. Raise the heat to moderate and stir-fry for 1 minute, mixing the pork thoroughly with the sauce and serve.

SLICED CHICKEN WITH WALNUTS

12 walnuts
6 oz. chicken breast
1 teaspoon salt
1 tablespoon cornflour
3 tablespoons lard
2 tablespoons leeks (thinly sliced)
1 tablespoon chopped onions
pepper to taste
½ teaspoon M.S.G.
1 teaspoon sesame oil

Shell the walnuts, blanch and remove membranes. Soak in fresh water for 1 hour. Drain and chop into peanut-sized pieces.

Cut the chicken into 6–8 thin slices. Rub in half the salt and half the cornflour.

Heat lard in a frying-pan over moderate heat. Add onion and leeks and stir-fry for ½ minute. Add walnuts and stir-fry together for 2½ minutes. Finally add chicken, pepper, remaining salt, M.S.G. and remaining cornflour blended in 1½ tablespoons water. Stir-fry for 1 minute, sprinkle with sesame oil and serve.

YUNNAN FISH CASSEROLE

2–3 lb. carp (bream, mullet)
1 teaspoon salt
4 Chinese dried mushrooms (soaked for 15 minutes and stems removed)
1 pair pork trotters
½ breakfast cup bamboo-shoots
3 oz. bacon (or ham)
2 tablespoons vegetable oil
1 clove garlic (crushed)
2 slices root ginger (chopped)
1 medium onion (sliced)
½ lb. celery (cut in 1 in. segments)
2 cakes bean curd (cut into 1 in. squares)

1 teaspoon dried shrimps
1 pint chicken broth
2 tablespoons soya sauce
2 tablespoons sherry
¼ teaspoon pepper
¼ teaspoon M.S.G.

Clean fish thoroughly and rub with salt inside and out. Simmer trotters gently in 1½ pints water for 1¼ hours. Slice the trotters and the bacon into slices 2 ins. × 1 in. × ¼ in. Add mushrooms and bamboo-shoots and continue to simmer for 20 minutes.

Heat oil in a large casserole. Add garlic, ginger and onion. Stir-fry together for 1½ minutes. Lay the fish in the oil and fry for 2 minutes on each side. Add celery, bean curd, dried shrimps and chicken broth, soya sauce, sherry, pepper and M.S.G. Bring to the boil, add the trotters, mushrooms, bamboo-shoots, and bacon and cover the casserole. Cook in an oven pre-heated to 375°F, gas 5, for half an hour. Serve in the casserole.

WU FAMILY SWEET DUMPLING BALLS

½ lb. glutinous rice flour (or ground glutinous rice)
⅓ pint warm water

for fillings

4 tablespoons sweetened bean paste (see p. 242)
1 tablespoon roasted sesame seeds mixed with 3 tablespoons brown sugar
3 tablespoons chopped crystallized fruit mixed with 1 tablespoon brown sugar

Add warm water gradually to flour and knead to a smooth dough. Form a long roll 1½ ins. in diameter. (If ground glutinous rice is used, allow dough to rest for 20 minutes.) Cut rounds about ¼ in. thick off the roll.

Mix the ingredients for the filling and place ½ tablespoon in the centre of each round of dough. Wrap dough around to form a firm ball. Make as many dumplings as the dough and filling will allow.

Either deep-fry the balls for 3½ minutes in hot oil, or simmer in 2½ pints of boiling water for 20 minutes. If they have been boiled serve the sweet dumplings in the water in which they were cooked, four or five to a bowl. This simple bland liquid is in refreshing contrast to the sweet filling and other savoury dishes.

If deep-fried, arrange the dumpling on a dish and sprinkle with a little sugar. Beware of the temperature of the filling!

Winter in Central China

Sweetbreads in Chicken Broth
Crispy Fish in Scrambled Egg
White Meat Balls in Crystal Consommé
Family Meal Bean Curd
Red-cooked Calves' Feet
Long-simmered Chicken with Tree-fungi
Little Red Heads

SWEETBREADS IN CHICKEN BROTH

8 oz. lamb's sweetbreads
½ chicken (approximately 1 lb.)
1 slice root ginger
1½ pints high broth (p. 90)
1 teaspoon salt
½ teaspoon M.S.G. (or ½ chicken stock cube)
1½ tablespoons sherry
½ tablespoon chives (chopped)

Clean sweetbreads and soak in a basin of water for 1 hour.

Drain and transfer to a pan of boiling water. Reduce heat and simmer for 15 minutes. Remove from pan and slice into ¼ in. slices. Arrange the slices neatly at the bottom of a deep dish.

Put chicken and ginger in a pan. Pour in the broth, cover and cook over moderate heat for 1 hour. Remove the chicken for another occasion. Sprinkle the sweetbreads with salt, M.S.G. and sherry. Pour over the concentrated broth and serve sprinkled with chopped chives.

CRISPY FISH IN SCRAMBLED EGG

½ lb. fresh sardines (or sprats)
6 eggs
2 spring onions (in 1 in. lengths)
½ teaspoon M.S.G.
1 teaspoon salt
vegetable oil for deep-frying
2 tablespoons lard
2 slices root ginger
1 medium onion (sliced)
3 tablespoons sherry

Clean fish thoroughly, rinse and drain.

Beat eggs for 10 seconds in a basin. Add spring onion, M.S.G., and half the salt and beat together for 5 seconds.

Heat oil in a deep-fryer. When very hot, lower in the fish in a wire basket for 3–4 minutes, until crisp. Remove and drain thoroughly.

Heat lard in a frying-pan, and stir-fry ginger and onion for ½ minute, then remove them with a perforated spoon. Pour in the beaten egg, tilting the pan so that the egg spreads over the base. Add the fish, spreading them over the egg. Sprinkle with remaining salt. Scramble them together and remove pan from fire. When the egg has cooked completely, place the pan over the fire again. Pour in the sherry and give a last short stir-fry. Dish out onto a warmed dish and serve. This is a strongly flavoured dish.

WHITE MEAT BALLS IN CRYSTAL CONSOMMÉ

9 oz. lean pork
3 oz. pork fat
1 egg (lightly beaten)
1½ teaspoons salt
½ teaspoon M.S.G. (or ½ chicken stock cube)
1 lb. cornflour (or water chestnut flour if available)
4 Chinese dried mushrooms (soaked and stems removed)
1 heart of spring greens (cut in four)
1 pint high broth (p. 90)
4 slices ham

Mince the pork meat and fat. Place in a basin and add beaten egg, 1 teaspoon salt, and the M.S.G. and mix well. Form the mixture into four large meat balls, and coat thoroughly with cornflour. Place them in a wire basket and dip them quickly into water. Drain, coat them again with cornflour. Repeat once more. Place the coated meat balls in a heatproof, deep serving dish. Surround with the mushrooms and greens, place in a steamer and steam vigorously for 40 minutes.

Heat broth in a pan, and, as soon as it boils, add remaining salt and pour it into the dish containing the meat balls. Add the slices of ham, steam for another 10 minutes and serve.

FAMILY MEAL BEAN CURD

4 bean curd cakes
3 oz. belly pork
4 tablespoons vegetable oil
2 teaspoons salted black beans (soaked in water 20 minutes, drained and chopped)
2 young leeks (cut in 1–1½ in. segments)
2 tablespoons chopped onion
2 dried chilli peppers

2 tablespoons soya sauce
4 tablespoons chicken broth
½ teaspoon M.S.G. (or ½ chicken stock cube)
2 teaspoons cornflour (blended in 2 tablespoons water)
1 tablespoon chopped chives
1 teaspoon sesame oil

Cut each bean curd cake into four. Slice pork into thin slices 2 ins. × 1½ ins.

Heat 3 tablespoons oil in a frying-pan. When hot, add the pieces of bean curd. Fry for 3 minutes gently turning the bean curd over a number of times. Remove and put aside.

Add remaining oil to the pan together with salted beans, onion, leek, pork and peppers. Stir-fry for 3 minutes. Pour in the soya sauce, broth and M.S.G.; stir-fry for 1 minute. Add cornflour, and stir until the liquid thickens. Return the bean curd to the pan, turn and mix with the other ingredients. Sprinkle with chopped chives and sesame oil and serve in a deep bowl.

RED-COOKED CALVES' FEET

1¼ lb. calves' feet
3 oz. cabbage heart (cut in 1½ in. squares)
2 tablespoons vegetable oil
2 tablespoons soya sauce
1 tablespoon oyster sauce
1 slice root ginger
pepper to taste
2 tablespoons dry sherry
¾ tablespoon cornflour (blended in 2 tablespoons water)
½ teaspoon M.S.G. (or ½ chicken stock cube)

Simmer calves' feet in 2 pints water in a heavy pan for 2½ hours, skimming as necessary. Remove and scrape off any inedible parts. Cut into 2 in. lengths. Reserve the cooking liquid.

Heat oil in a saucepan. When hot, add cabbage and stir-fry for 1½ minutes over moderate heat. Return the calves' feet to the pan. Add soya sauce, oyster sauce, ginger, sherry, pepper and 1 cup of cooking liquid. Stir once or twice. Cover and simmer for 10 minutes. Turn calves' feet over and simmer for another 10 minutes. Add cornflour and M.S.G. Stir gently until liquid thickens. Serve in a deep dish or casserole.

LONG-SIMMERED CHICKEN WITH TREE-FUNGI

4 tablespoons white tree-fungi
10 oz. chicken breast
1 tablespoon cornflour
1 egg-white
½ teaspoon salt
½ teaspoon M.S.G.
1 tablespoon parsley (chopped)

Soak fungi in warm water for 1 hour and clean thoroughly. Cut chicken meat into thin slices 1½ ins. × 1 in. Beat egg-white for 10 seconds and mix well with cornflour to make a paste. Coat the chicken evenly with the paste.

Heat 1 pint of water in a large saucepan. When it starts to boil add the chicken. Keep the pieces apart with a perforated spoon or pair of chopsticks. Simmer for 5 minutes, then pour away a quarter of the water.

Pour the chicken and remaining water into a casserole. Simmer over low heat for 5 minutes. Spread the fungi on top of the chicken. Sprinkle with salt and M.S.G. Cover the casserole, and place it in a pre-heated oven at 350°F, gas 4, for ¾ hour. Serve in the casserole, sprinkled with chopped parsley.

LITTLE RED HEADS

½ lb. plain flour
¼ teaspoon salt
½ breakfast cup water
1 oz. pork fat
1 oz. bread (in rice grain-sized crumbs)

1 oz. chopped dates
1 oz. crystallized fruit (chopped)
2½ oz. sugar
red food colouring powder (small quantity)

Mix flour, salt, and water in basin. Knead into a dough. Form into a long roll about 1½ in. in diameter. Cut off slices ¼ in. thick. Roll out on a floured board into thin rounds about 3 ins. in diameter.

Boil the pork fat for 15 minutes, then drain and dice into pieces the size of rice grains. Mix pork fat, bread, sugar, and fruit together well. Place a dessertspoon of this filling at the centre of each dough round, and shape into round cones with a point at the top. Arrange these sweet-filled cones on a heatproof dish. Place in a steamer and steam for 15 minutes.

Touch each tip with a dab of red food colouring. These sweets can be eaten steamed, or they can be deep-fried for 2–3 minutes and served crisp. Little red heads are a great favourite with the Chinese masses.

Traditional Specialities

Peking Duck
Bird's Nest Soup

Braised Shark's Fin with Crab
Peking Sliced Lamb Hot-pot
First Rank Hot-pot
Chrysanthemum Hot-pot
Eight Jewel Rice

There are a number of traditional Chinese dishes which should not be overlooked if we are to make a reasonably complete survey of Chinese cuisine. As several of these were not included in the preceding sections, they follow here.

PÉKING DUCK

Peking Duck is a world-famous dish, which is, in fact, simple to cook. The following procedure is one of the simplest. It should be noted that Peking Duck has achieved its justifiable fame, not only because of the way it is prepared, but also because of the way it is eaten, wrapped in a pancake – a procedure which is described below, after the recipe:

1 duck (3–4 lb.)
1 teaspoon malt sugar
2 tablespoons soya sauce
1 dozen pancakes (see p. 237)
½ cucumber
10 spring onions
8 tablespoons plum sauce
8 tablespoons sweet bean paste jam (see p. 242 or hoisin sauce)

Clean the duck thoroughly and place it in a basin. Boil a large kettle of water and pour it over the duck, dousing it thoroughly. Remove and dry the bird immediately and thoroughly (with paper towel). Hang it by the neck to dry overnight in an airy place.

Melt malt sugar in soya sauce, and rub the duck with this

mixture. When this coating has dried, place it on a wire rack in a preheated oven at 375°F, gas 5, to roast for exactly 1 hour. Do not baste or open the oven door.

First slice off the crisp skin in 1–2 in. squares, and then slice the meat off the duck. Place them on two separate warmed dishes and bring to table. They are eaten wrapped in pancakes, with a liberal spread of plum sauce, or bean paste jam, together with a few segments of spring onion, and a few thin strips of cucumber, about 2 ins. long. The sauce, the jam, the spring onions and cucumber should all be laid out in separate small dishes. After the duck carcass has been stripped of its meat it is normally boiled up with a large amount of cabbage and is traditionally served as a soup to end the meal.

BIRD'S NEST SOUP

What could be a more exotic dish than a bird's nest! Prepared as a soup, as it normally is, it actually does not taste particularly unfamiliar because of the familiar ingredients used: chicken, egg white, ham, etc. The rarer bird's nests are small and cup-shaped, but the more ordinary types are in the form of porous brittle cakes, which need to be soaked.

5 oz. bird's nest
4–5 oz. chicken breast
2 oz. ham
2 tablespoons dry sherry
2 breakfast cups chicken broth
2 egg whites
½ teaspoon salt
1 spring onion (finely chopped)

Soak bird's nest overnight in water. Drain and clean, picking out any feathers with tweezers, if necessary. Simmer gently in water for 20 minutes. Leave it to stand, drain and cool.

Meanwhile, mince chicken and ham and keep separate. Mix minced chicken with sherry and 2 tablespoons broth. Beat egg whites lightly, blend with the chicken mixture and beat together for 5–6 seconds.

Add remaining chicken broth to the bird's nest in a saucepan. Add salt and spring onion and bring to the boil, simmering gently for 10 minutes. Now slide the chicken and egg-white mixture in slowly along the prongs of a fork. Stir, sprinkle with ham, and serve.

Although the bird's nest has a subtle flavour, it is the lightly cooked minced chicken which provides most of the fresh flavour.

BRAISED SHARK'S FIN WITH CRAB

Shark's fin is really another of those dishes where the appeal lies principally in its rarity value and exotic background. Otherwise (this may be blasphemy), it is not unlike well-prepared calves' feet!

2½ lb. raw shark's fin
3 slices root ginger
2 pints bone broth
1 pint strong chicken broth
1 cup red-cooked meat gravy
4 oz. white crab meat
1 tablespoon lard
1 tablespoon finely chopped ham
2 tablespoons dry sherry

Soak the shark's fin overnight in water. Scrape and clean away any attached bone or dried meat. Place in a pan of water, bring to the boil, then simmer for 3 hours. Remove, scrape and clean for a second time. Put in a saucepan of fresh boiling water and simmer with 1 slice of root ginger for 1 hour. Discard the water and ginger and repeat once more with a fresh slice of ginger. Discard this water and ginger and add bone broth and the third slice of root ginger; simmer for 2 hours. Pour away the broth and ginger.

Place the fin in a casserole. Add chicken broth and simmer for 1 hour. Now add meat gravy and most of the crab meat and simmer for a further ½ hour.

Finally place the fin and gravy in a deep heatproof dish. Add lard, sprinkle with ham and sherry, and garnish with the remaining crab meat. Steam for 15 minutes and serve.

Hot-pots

There are many hot-pot recipes in China; most large cities, provinces or regions can boast one. The main basic difference is between the red hot-pot in which soya sauce is used, and the white, in which it is not. It is hardly worth serving a hot-pot for less than six people, and the recipes which follow give sufficient quantities for anything from six to ten people.

Two types of pots are used: the funnelled, charcoal-burning type, sometimes called a Peking hot-pot, and the wide, flat-bottomed type which burns methylated spirit, sometimes known as a Chrysanthemum Hot-pot. (This name is derived from chrysanthemum petals which are used as a garnish over the contents.)

All the materials for the meal, thinly sliced and uncooked, may be provided in small saucer-sized dishes and cooked at the table itself.

Alternatively, the ingredients can be cooked or partly cooked beforehand, and packed neatly by type in different parts of the pot for the cooking to be completed in the clear consommé in which they are immersed. This latter method of entertaining is more usual for a meal consisting of a number of courses, though many people prefer the more informal do-it-yourself meals. All hot-pots are meant for six to ten people.

PEKING SLICED LAMB HOT-POT

Peking Sliced Lamb Hot-pot is a well-known dish which is usually treated as a meal in itself.

Like many Peking dishes which have a Chinese Moslem grassland background, the materials and ingredients of this Hot-pot are simple and straightforward.

(for 6–10 people)

4 lb. lamb (leg or shoulder)
1½ lb. celery cabbage (or tender leaves of Savoy cabbage)
3 oz. transparent pea-starch noodles
¼ lb. spinach (thoroughly cleaned)
1¼ pints bone broth
1¼ pints chicken broth
1 teaspoon salt

for dips and mixes

good quality soya sauce
hoisin sauce
choppped chives
chopped garlic
chopped root ginger
chilli sauce
vinegar
sherry
tomato sauce
mustard

Cut lamb into razor-thin slices about 1 in. × 4 ins. (about 12 slices per lb.) Add 1 pint of each type of broth to the hot-pot and cover. Fan up the charcoal burning in the fat squat funnel before bringing the hot-pot to the table. The soup in the hot-pot should be boiling vigorously shortly after it comes to the table.

When the broth is boiling vigorously about a quarter of the vegetables and noodles are put in to begin to cook. At this point the guests will be busy mixing their dips to their own taste in individual bowls from the various sauces and ingredients which are laid out on the table.

When the pot comes back to the boil, each guest puts in his own portion of lamb using his chopsticks. He pushes a slice or two of lamb into the boiling broth, generally for no longer than 1 minute. As soon as the meat is cooked, he retrieves it from the broth with his chopsticks, together with some vegetables and noodles. He dips these in his own dip before eating. This continues until nearly all the meat and vegetables have been eaten. Then, for the last round all the remaining broth, meat and vegetables are added to the pot, and the lid put on firmly. Within a few moments the contents will come to the boil again; after two to three minutes the lid is taken off and the remaining meat, vegetables and broth are ladled out into individual bowls and eaten. This is very warming in the Peking winter!

For a hearty meal, each person should be provided with at least a pound of lamb; he should also have a raw egg to poach in the broth, or beat up in a bowl and use as a dip for the meat as soon as it comes out of the hot-pot and before it is dipped into the mixed sauces.

Steamed buns or unleavened bread can be eaten with lamb. But as often as not the lamb is eaten on its own, except for what is cooked in the hot-pot (which increases proportionately with the quantity of lamb).

FIRST RANK HOT-POT

The Peking hot-pot just described is called a First Rank Hot-pot, if, instead of the raw lamb being cooked at the table, the pot is packed with various cooked and half-cooked foods, all covered with a consommé, allowed to cook for a few minutes in the kitchen, and brought to the table with the lid on. The

Shih Chin or Ten Variety Hot-pot has approximately ten ingredients, usually chosen from the following:

chicken	fish balls
duck	shrimps (or scallops, oysters etc.)
pork shoulder	bean curd (pre-fried)
hard–boiled eggs	dried mushrooms (soaked)
ham	celery cabbage
liver (chicken, duck, pork)	spinach
bamboo-shoots	transparent pea-starch noodles

The amount of food depends upon the size of the hot-pot, and what is available or in season. A rough guide is 3–4 oz. of each ingredient, (enough for 6–10 people), except for the mushrooms, of which 2 oz. will be sufficient, as they are strong. As much as 6–8 oz. of spinach or cabbage can be included. With the Peking funnelled hot-pot, the food is neatly packed in sections around the moat which surrounds the funnel. When the 'moat' is full, the broth, which can be quite dilute, is poured in. Naturally, the broth is enriched by all the ingredients which are cooked in it.

The different foods have to be pre-cooked for different lengths of time before they are put in the hot-pot: the pork for 20 minutes or more; the duck and liver for 10 minutes; chicken, fish balls and shrimps for 5 minutes; the vegetables will have to be blanched or parboiled for 2–3 minutes, noodles and mushrooms need only be soaked, and the bean curd cakes will have to be fried for a couple of minutes. The pot is put to cook for 7–8 minutes in the kitchen and when it is brought to the dining table, it only requires a few more minutes cooking. As the cooking proceeds, different ingredients and additional broths can be added at any time, or the seasoning can be adjusted. The main thing is to keep the hot-pot alight, simmering and bubbling throughout the meal. Eventually, as with the preceding recipe, a very rich and savoury soup is produced, which is drunk with great satisfaction towards the end of the meal, after many other dishes have been eaten.

CHRYSANTHEMUM HOT-POT

Chrysanthemum Hot-pot is much the same as the previous hot-pot, except that a round, wide, flat-bottomed basin (usually brass) with a lid is generally used. The pot sits on a raised frame on top of a methylated-spirit burner.

The ingredients are not packed side by side in the round, flat-bottomed pot, but in orderly layers from the bottom up. Although there need not be any precise order, traditionally, the bottom layer is cabbage, then fried bean curd, followed by chicken and meat, and eventually ending up with fish balls on top. The main thing when experimenting with this dish is to pack the different layers of food in neatly. If you want to be really authentic, you can strew a few chrysanthemum petals over the food before it is brought to the table.

The main difference between the northern and southern hot-pots is that, in the former, meats predominate, while in the latter more seafoods are used.

EIGHT JEWEL RICE

Eight Jewel Rice is really a pudding, like a Christmas pudding, studded with a variety of nuts, preserves, and crystallized fruit, and made by alternating thick layers of sweetened rice, thin layers of sweetened bean paste, nuts and fruits. For westerners who are used to making desserts, this Chinese rice pudding should be simple!

1 lb. glutinous rice
½ cup suet
5 tablespoons lard

6 tablespoons sugar
3 tablespoons glacé cherries
3 tablespoons crystallized orange peel
4 tablespoons dates
4 tablespoons lotus seeds (or raw peanuts)
2 tablespoons melon seeds
4 tablespoons dragon's eyes (*loong ngaan*)
3 tablespoons other crystallized fruits
4 tablespoons walnuts
2 tablespoons almonds
8 tablespoons sweetened bean paste

Bring rice to boil in 1¼ pints of water, and simmer very gently until it is dry. Mix in all the suet and the sugar. Allow them to simmer over very gentle heat for another 5–6 minutes.

Blanch lotus seeds, almonds, walnuts, and stone the dates. Break the larger nuts into smaller pieces.

Grease a basin or mould heavily with lard. Arrange the preserved fruits, nuts, and seeds in attractive colour patterns at the bottom of the basin, and press them through the lard so that they will show when the pudding is cooked and unmoulded. Do the same on the sides of the basin. Spoon in and pack down layers of glutinous rice, alternating with thin layers of bean paste. Press the rice down so the pudding will hold its shape when turned out.

Place the basin in a steamer (or in a pot placed inside a large saucepan a quarter full of water), and steam for 1½ hours.

When ready, turn the pudding out just as you would a Christmas pudding, by pressing the serving plate against the rice, and inverting both the basin and plate together in one action.

Eight Jewel Rice with all its colourful nuts and fruits is an attractive pudding. It should be eaten hot.

Snacks and Miscellanies

Stuffed Steamed Buns or *Pao-tzu*
Dumpling Pouches or *Chiao-tzu*
Paper-wrapped Chicken
Crispy Prawn Toast
Pancakes for Peking Duck and Other Types of Roast
Meat

As already mentioned in an earlier chapter, savoury snacks
play quite a large part in Chinese life, since those who can
afford it spend a good deal of their time in recreational
eating.

There must be a dozen categories of savoury snacks, but the
most important are:

steamed buns or *pao-tzu*
steamed or boiled dumpling pouches or *chiao-tzu*
fried crispies
fried noodles or chow mein

Then there are *yuan hsiaos* (sweet filled dumplings p. 56), soup noodles (eaten as meals on their own), steamed bundles, the pies – *feng kuos* – of Canton, and the various savoury *congees* (soft-rice), which are so far removed from western life and western traditions that it is scarcely worth trying to acquire a taste for them, or engineering their faithful reproduction in a western kitchen.

We have already dealt in detail with fried noodles (*chow mein* p. 51), fried rice (*chow fan* p. 55), spring or pancake rolls (*choong chuan* p. 53). We shall now describe some of the other items.

There are really only two types of steamed buns or *pao-tzu*: those with savoury fillings, and those with sweet.

STEAMED BUNS OR PAO-TZU

1 lb. flour
1½ teaspoons dried yeast
½ pint water
1 tablespoon sugar

Dissolve the yeast in 4 tablespoons of warm water and add to the flour in a basin. Add the remaining water gradually. Knead well for 7–8 minutes. Leave the dough to stand in a warm place for a couple of hours, then knead again for 2–3 minutes.

Shape the dough into a roll 2 foot long and 2 ins. in diameter. Slice the roll into rounds 1 in. thick. Place a tablespoon of filling at the centre of each round, and draw the sides up to a point enclosing the filling completely. In this way each round is made into a flat-bottomed ball with a slightly pointed top, about 2½ ins. high. Place a number of these at a time in a steamer on a piece of cheesecloth, and steam vigorously for 25 minutes.

The fillings for the steamed buns can be made from fresh as

well as cooked foods – usually a combination of the two. The following are fairly typical fillings:

(A) 1 lb. coarsely minced pork
   3 young leeks (chopped)
   2 spring onions (chopped)
   1 teaspoon salt
   2 teaspoons sugar
   1 tablespoon soya sauce
   1 teaspoon sesame oil

(B) 1 lb. *cha hao* pork (p. 94; cut into very small slices)
   1 onion (chopped)
   2 spring onions (chopped)
   1 clove garlic (chopped)
   2½ tablespoons soya sauce
   2 teaspoons sugar
   1 teaspoon sesame oil

Mix all the ingredients for each filling well in a basin, and allow them to stand for 1–1½ hours before using.

Sweet fillings

(C) 1 lb. black bean purée
   ½ lb. sugar
   4 tablespoons lard

(D) 6 oz. ground walnuts
   2 oz. sesame seeds
   1 oz. pork fat (minced)
   ½ lb. sugar
   2 tablespoons lard

Fry the ingredients for each filling together for 5 minutes over gentle heat. Allow them to stand and cool for 1 hour before using.

Pao-tzu are meant to be eaten on their own, like hot sandwiches.

There are two other varieties of steamed buns which are meant to accompany savoury or very rich foods, such as meat with plenty of gravy; indeed, they improve such meat. They are called *man-tou* which are plain buns and *hua-chuen*, flower rolls or fancy rolls.

The dough for making *man-tou* is exactly the same as that for steamed buns, except that the sugar is omitted. The only difference is that no filling is wrapped inside. Each round of dough is simply made into a round flat-bottomed bun and steamed for 18–20 minutes.

The dough for flower rolls is also the same. However the procedure is different: when the dough is ready, it is divided in two. Each portion is then rolled into a sheet ⅛ in. thick. Each sheet is then sprinkled with ½ teaspoon salt and brushed with 1 tablespoon vegetable oil (or sesame oil, if available). Place one sheet on top of the other – the oiled surface against the non-oiled. Then roll the two sheets up together into a long roll about 2 ins. in diameter. Trim off the end bits and cut the roll into pieces 3 ins. long. Press the middle of each length with a fork or a pair of chopsticks so that the ends open out slightly more.

Steam the flower rolls vigorously on cheese cloth for 18–20 minutes.

The flower rolls are more elegant versions of the plain rolls and are used on festive occasions. The plain rolls are just daily bread to the northern Chinese, though steamed rather than baked.

DUMPLING POUCHES OR CHIAO-TZU

Chiao-tzu, which are meat fillings wrapped in thin dough made of flour and water without any raising agent, should be made and eaten in large numbers. The fillings can also be sweet, but are usually savoury.

The dough is made by mixing ½ pint of water with 3 times its volume of flour. Knead until very smooth. Cover with a damp cloth and allow to stand for half an hour. Then form the dough into a long roll with a diameter of about 1 in.

Cut the roll into rounds ½ in. thick. Roll each round out on a floured board into a thin sheet about 3½ ins. in diameter. Place a teaspoonful of filling in the centre. The bottom edge of the skin is then pulled over the filling; the top edge is puckered and then folded over to meet the bottom edge, they are sealed by pressing together.

The dumpling pouches are usually boiled or steamed. The timing for boiling is measured by a technique called 're-boiling'. The dumpling pouches are put into a large pan of boiling water (6–8 pints). You wait for it to come back to the boil, let it boil for 10 seconds and then add another ½ pint of water. Again wait for it to come back to the boil, and after 10 seconds again pour in another ½ pint of water. Repeat this three times and the *chiao-tzu* are ready.

They are then drained and eaten dipped in soya sauce or vinegar.

In Canton these dumplings are made in round, squat shapes with an open top and are called *hsiao mai*. They are often partly stuffed with seafood. The dumpling pouches can be put in a greased pan and allowed to fry for 5–6 minutes until the bottoms are brown. The tops are sprinkled once or twice with water or a mixture of water and vinegar. These so-called *kuo tieh* (or 'stuck to the pot') – are a great favourite in Peking. They should be juicy inside, soft on top, and crisp underneath.

There are two types of fried crisp savouries which are well worth trying, namely paper-wrapped chicken, and crispy prawn toast.

PAPER-WRAPPED CHICKEN

I do not know if cooking in cellophane paper is unique to China, but it certainly produces very tasty results. In China it is limited to a comparatively small number of variations – paper-wrapped chicken being the best known.

6 oz. chicken (shredded into 30 pieces)
2 spring onions (in 1½ in. lengths)
2 stalks celery (blanched and cut in 1½ in. lengths)
4 Chinese dried mushrooms (soaked for 20 minutes, stems removed, sliced into matchstick strips)
1 tablespoon chicken fat
1½ tablespoons oyster sauce
1½ tablespoons sherry
1½ tablespoons soya sauce
½ teaspoon M.S.G.
1 slice root ginger (finely chopped)
1 large sheet cellophane paper
oil for deep-frying
2 teaspoons sugar

Mix the chicken fat, oyster sauce, sherry, sugar, soya sauce, M.S.G. and root ginger in a basin, and put in the chicken to marinate for 1 hour. Cut cellophane paper into pieces 3 ins. wide by 2 ins. long.

Place two pieces of marinated chicken, lengthwise, just below the centre of each piece of cellophane paper. Lay on them a segment of spring onion, and a piece of celery (also lengthwise). Add a few mushroom strips. Roll up the ingredients tightly from the bottom. About 1 in. from the top of the cellophane paper, turn in about ½ in. at the two sides, folding them over firmly. Finally turn down the top of the cellophane paper, and tuck the flap in firmly underneath the turned-in ends, (if necessary place a small weight on top to keep the 'envelope' flat while you are making the others). When they are all made, line them up side by side, like a tray full of unopened letters.

Heat up the oil in the deep-fryer. Place 5 or 6 'envelopes' in a wire basket, and lower them into very hot oil to fry for 2 minutes. Drain, put aside and keep hot, while you fry the others. When they have all been fried once, put them all together in the wire basket, and fry them all for 2 minutes more, by which time the contents will be well and truly cooked. Drain the envelopes quickly and thoroughly, arrange them on a warmed dish and serve.

The guests each pick out an envelope with chopsticks and open it on their own plates. Because the food is enclosed until the moment of eating nothing is lost of its heat, aroma and flavour.

CRISPY PRAWN TOAST

6 oz. prawns
4 oz. fillet of fish
2 eggs
½ teaspoon salt
pepper (to taste)
½ lb. breadcrumbs
3 tablespoons sesame seeds
2 tablespoons chopped parsley
4 large slices of bread
oil for deep-frying

Remove the crust from the slices of bread and toast them until they just begin to colour. Cut each slice into six fingers.

Chop the prawns and fish into a paste, add salt, pepper and 3 teaspoons of beaten egg to bind. Mix well together in a basin. Place the remaining beaten egg in another basin. Mix the breadcrumbs and sesame seeds and spread them out on a large plate or tray.

Spread each piece of bread with a thick layer of prawn-fish paste. Dip them quickly in the beaten egg, then coat thickly with breadcrumbs and sesame seeds. When all the little pieces of bread have been spread, dipped, and coated, arrange them separately in a wire basket, 5 or 6 at a time and deep-fry in hot oil for 2 minutes. Drain, put aside and keep hot. (As soon as the coated bread is put into the hot oil all the components will hold firm.) When all twenty-four pieces of crispy prawn toast are ready, place them all together in the wire basket, and fry for 1 final minute. Drain them quickly, decorate each piece with a small spray of parsley, and serve on a warmed dish.

PANCAKES FOR PEKING DUCK AND OTHER ROAST MEATS

The pancakes are not self-contained, but an essential accompaniment to many well-known meat dishes. Four main types of 'bulk-food' are used to absorb the richness of meat dishes: boiled rice, *man-tou*, flower rolls, and pancakes. These pancakes differ from those used in pancake rolls mainly by being smaller and drier (no egg being used).

2 cups flour
1 cup boiling water
small quantity vegetable oil (or sesame oil)

Boil water and add gradually to flour in a basin. Mix well with a wooden spoon, but do not knead. Cover with a cloth and leave to stand for 20 minutes.

Form the dough into a long roll about 2 ins. in diameter. Cut off ½ in. rounds from the roll. Roll the rounds into balls and flatten again into round cakes ¼ in. thick. Brush the tops of the cakes lightly with oil, and place them in pairs one on top of the other, with the oiled surface together.

When you have used up the dough, dust each pair of cakes with flour and roll them out into paper-thin pancakes. Place each pair over low heat in a heavy ungreased frying-pan and cook for 1¼ minutes on each side. They are ready when parts of the pancake start to curl and bubble slightly; tear them gently apart, stack them and cover with a damp cloth until required. Alternatively, store in a refrigerator, and steam for 7–8 minutes before use.

Dips and Mixes

Apart from sauces which are poured straight out of bottles into saucers and put on the table, dips are often mixed by the guests in individual bowls from a choice of ingredients which are provided at the table.

Usually there will be small bowls containing soya sauce, plum sauce, tomato sauce, chilli sauce, vinegar, sherry, and prepared mustard laid out ready when a dish traditionally eaten with a dip is to be served.

The proportions of the different constituents is obviously a matter of individual preference, but the following gives a rough guide:

Soya-Chilli Dip

4 units soya sauce
2 units chilli sauce

Soya-Garlic Dip

4 tablespoons soya sauce
2 cloves garlic (crushed)

Tomato-Soya-Chilli Dip

4 units tomato sauce
4 units soya sauce
1 unit chilli sauce

Soya-Sherry Dip

Equal quantities sherry and soya sauce

Soya-Mustard Dip

4 units soya sauce
2 units prepared mustard
   (English)

Chilli-Vinegar Dip

4 units wine vinegar
1 unit chilli oil
4 units salad oil

Tangerine Dip

Equal quantities tangerine juice and olive oil

The following two mixes require cooking and are prepared in the kitchen and brought ready made to the table.

Salt and Pepper Mix

2 teaspoons pepper
2 tablespoons salt

Mix the salt and pepper and heat them on a pre-heated absolutely dry pan for 1½–2 minutes over low heat. This quantity is sufficient to divide between two saucers.

Sweet and Sour Sauce (Basic)

1½ tablespoons soya sauce
1½ tablespoons sugar
1½ tablespoons vinegar
1 tablespoon tomato sauce
1 tablespoon dry sherry
¾ tablespoon cornflour (blended in 4 tablespoons water)

Mix all the ingredients in a bowl till quite smooth. Heat the mixture gently in a small saucepan till it thickens. Pour into two small bowls.

Chinese Ingredients and Possible Substitutes

Substitutes
(where available)

Abalone (or awabi)

A smooth-textured shellfish, usually available dried or canned. Used extensively for flavouring – in soups, red-cooking or mixed frying.

Agar-agar

A dried seaweed, comes in thin strips. Must be soaked and used as gelatine.

Unflavoured gelatine.

Anise-star

Brown, dried, star-shaped cloves. Used to flavour red-cooked poultry and meat dishes. Only small quantities are used at a time.

Cinnamon.

Bamboo-shoots

Crunchy, ivory-coloured shoots of bamboo, usually cut as they emerge from the ground. They have a texture similar to many root vegetables. Add sweetness and delicacy and a variation in texture. Usually canned, and should be rinsed before use. The dried variety is often used for flavouring meat, fish, and vegetable dishes. Needs to be soaked.

Cabbage or carrot can be used to substitute for texture.

Bean Curd

Smooth, cream-coloured purée of soya beans, which has been pressed and set into cakes approximately 3 ins. square and 1 in. thick. It is highly nutritious and is used extensively in Chinese cooking as a vegetable. Itself bland, it is extremely useful in absorbing and harmonizing the flavour of other ingredients, whether meats, seafoods or vegetables, both dried and fresh. It is one of the most important of Chinese foods. It is usually available fresh from Chinese foodstores (sold in cakes), but is also available canned.

Bean Curd Cheese

Comes in small cream or red-coloured cakes. Salty and highly savoury. Like chilli oil, you should adjust the quantity of bean curd cheese in a recipe to suit your own taste. If you find it too strong and salty, use slightly less. Used as a flavourer in cooking or eaten with bland foods (*congee* or rice-porridge). Sold canned or in jars.

Bean Jam or *Sweetened Bean Paste*

Brownish-black paste, normally used in desserts as filling or spread. Can be made by frying 4 tablepoons unsalted bean paste with 1½ tablespoons sugar, 1½ tablespoons lard and 1 teaspoon sesame oil. Stir over low heat for 4–5 minutes until mixture is smooth. (Also see p. 157.)

Chopped or mashed dates

Bean Paste

A salty brown paste, which can be used instead of soya sauce wherever a thicker sauce is required. Sold canned or in jars.

Bean Sprouts

Tiny off-white shoots of mung beans (or peas). Very crunchy, can be stir-fried with most meats and vegetables. They are grown by most Chinese restaurants (can be grown at any time of the year indoors in a few days), but are usually available by weight from Chinese food-stores. The canned types are too mushy and not recommended.

Black Beans

Salted and fermented black beans give a salty strong taste to fish, seafoods and meat. Usually used in steaming or stir-frying in conjunction with these foods. Sold in packets or by weight.

French capers.

Bêche-de-Mer

Also called sea-cucumber or sea-slug. Comes in dried, black banana-shaped pieces, 3–6 ins. long. Must be soaked overnight. When soaked becomes gela-tinous and is usually cooked with meat and poultry and served as a delicacy at banquets.

Bird's Nest

From the nests of sea-swallows – they are not the nests themselves, but dried gelatinous coating in the nests, produced by the birds. They are beige and come in three forms: small shallow cups, chips or broken cups, and porous fragments. They are sold in small boxes by weight. They must be soaked and cleaned before use. They are usually made into soup (in chicken broth) or cooked with sugar crystals into a sweet dish.

Chinese Cabbage

A vegetable with long, smooth, white stems, which resembles a cross between celery and cabbage. It has a delicate flavour and crunchy texture. It can be cooked with most meats, poultry and seafoods. Available all the year round in China. Often available in the U.S. and beginning to be seen in the U.K.

Celery or Savoy cabbage

Pickled Cabbage

Usually yellow-greenish in colour soaked in brine and packed in jars. Often called in Chinese 'Winter Vegetables' (or Doan Choy). It is usually chopped or sliced for use. Adds tang to steamed and stir-fried dishes. It is also available canned. Needs to be rinsed before use.

Sauerkraut plus salt.

Salted Cabbage

Pungent, and greenish-brown in colour. Available in bundles. Used for flavouring meat, fish and soup. Must be soaked or rinsed and chopped before use.

Szechuan Cabbage

Comes in tins and is salty and very hot.

Add 1 tablespoon paprika to 2 lb. salted cabbage and leave for 2 days.

Chilli Sauce

Hot, red sauce. Comes in bottles.

Tabasco sauce.

Chilli oil

Red transparent liquid, bought in small bottles. Very hot, must use sparingly.

Chilli sauce or Tabasco sauce

Dragon's Eyes (Loong Ngaan)

These are like small lichees with similar succulent flesh and a round pip in the middle. They are obtainable canned from Chinese foodstores.

Egg (Ancient or 1,000-year-old)

These eggs have been called '1,000-year-old' because they appear to have been dug out of the ground by archaeologists. They are really unshelled pickled eggs, which have been buried in earth, lime and chopped straw for 1–2 months. When shelled their insides are dark, pungent, and savoury. Eat with soft rice or as hors d'oeuvres.

Five-Spice Powder

A coffee-coloured ready-mixed powder containing star anise, anise pepper, fennel, cloves, and cinnamon. It is very strong and pungent. Seldom more than a quarter of a teaspoon is used at a time to season red-cooked meats and poultry. Sold in packets or by weight.

Ginger (root)

Root ginger is a small potato-like root, with a wrinkled yellow skin. Used extensively with meat, poultry, and fish. Adds sharpness to taste. Only small quantity used at a time. Sold by weight. Use the fresh root not the dried white variety or the powder. Will keep for several months in a polythene bag.

Dried ginger.

Ginkgo Nuts

Also called 'white-nuts'. Used in soups and long-cooked meat and poultry dishes. Need to be shelled and blanched. Available canned.

Small new potatoes.

Glutinous Rice and Ground Glutinous Rice

Used for stuffings and sweet dishes. Requires soaking for 20 minutes before cooking. Becomes sticky when cooked. Obtainable in packets or by weight from Chinese foodstores.

Round grain rice, or 'pudding rice'. Pound in a mortar for ground glutinous rice.

Golden Needles (Lily Buds)

Long, dried strips, golden yellow in colour. Require soaking before cooking. Always used in conjunction with other materials, meats or vegetables. Have a unique, musty taste. Sold in bundles by weight.

Lotus Leaves

The leaves of the water-lily plant, usually dried and used for wrapping foods for cooking. They make the foods very fragrant. They require soaking before use. Available from most Chinese food stores.

Lotus Seeds

Seeds of the water-lily plant, used both in desserts and meat dishes.

Raw unsalted peanuts

Lotus Roots

The roots of the water-lily measuring about 2 ins. in diameter. They have a crunchy texture and are used sliced as a vegetable. Dried variety are supplied by Chinese food stores in packages or by weight. Also available canned.

Pineapple.

Melon Seeds

Available from Chinese foodstores.

Chinese Mushrooms

Chinese mushrooms are almost always dried. They are brownish-black in colour and require soaking (15–30 minutes) before use. They are much stronger and more distinctive in taste than fresh mushrooms. Sold by weight. Expensive.

Dried mushrooms.

M.S.G. (*Gourmet-Powder, Flavour Powder*)

See p. 9, Author's note. Usually available in small tins.

Chicken stock cube.

Mung Beans (or Peas)

Small dried green peas, used for growing bean sprouts or made into pea-starch noodles. Sold by weight.

Transparent Noodles
(pea starch or cellophane noodles)

These are white and semi-transparent. Need to be soaked before cooking. Can be used in stir-fried 'assembled' or long-cooked dishes. They absorb gravies and other flavours very well. Sold in bundles and by weight.

Sesame Oil

A nutty flavoured oil, used in small quantities for its aromatic qualities. Usually sold in bottles.

Sesame Seeds

Tiny flat seeds, usually used roasted to give aroma to cakes and desserts. Sold by weight.

Sesame Jam

Bought in Chinese food stores, has a pronounced nutty flavour.

2 teaspoons sesame oil stirred into 3 tablespoons peanut butter.

SAUCES

Oyster Sauce

A thick greyish-brown liquid made from oysters and soya sauce, used for flavouring meats and poultry. Sold in bottles.

Shrimp Sauce

A highly savoury, anchovy-like dark golden liquid, used for general flavouring in cooking. Used occasionally in dips. Sold in bottles.

Hoisin Sauce

A thick brownish-red spicy vegetable-based sauce. Used for flavouring, especially vegetables, shellfish, duck and spare ribs. Sold in jars and cans.

Plum Sauce

A chutney-like sauce, made from plums, apricot, chilli, vinegar and sugar. Usually used as a dip for roast meat dishes. Sold in jars.

Chutney.

Soya Sauce

A salty light or dark brown sauce, which adds flavour to meat, poultry, fish, and vegetables. It is also served as a dip in a small sauce dish on the table. The dark sauce is stronger and thicker than the light, which is usually confined to Canton.

Chinese Sausage or Salami

A dried salami-like sausage, which is sweet and salty. Comes tied in pairs or bundles. Can be steamed or quick-fried, usually combined with other foods.

Dried Italian salami.

Shark's Fin

Hard, dried pieces of cartilage, greyish-brown in colour. Needs prolonged soaking and cooking. When cooked becomes translucent. Usually braised or cooked in thick soup. Considered a delicacy in China. Sold by weight or in boxes. Expensive.

Rock Sugar

Amber-coloured sugar crystals, used for sweetening desserts and sweet teas. Sold by weight.

Sugar.

Malt Sugar

Used mixed with soya sauce to give colour and crispness to skins of roasts. Sold in jars or cans.

Sugar.

Dried Squid

Can be bought in dark brown sheets about 6 ins. × 10 ins.

Use the same quantity of smoked haddock as squid, adding 1 teaspoon anchovy per ¼ lb. haddock.

Tangerine Peel

Called *Chen-pi* in Chinese. Comes in small pieces about 2 ins. square. For short cooking they should be soaked for 20–30 minutes. You can make your own by drying tangerine peels in an oven at 250°F, gas 2, for ½ hour. Store in a screw top jar. Double the quantity of peel in a recipe if you are using homemade, instead of bought, peel.

Tree-fungi (Wood-ears)

These fungi are ear-like in shape when soaked. They have a very slippery and

crunchy texture. and are greyish in
colour. They are used most often in stir-
fried and assembled dishes.

Wine Sediment Paste

Difficult to obtain in the West. See p. 37
and p. 165 for recipes for an acceptable
substitute.

Some Chinese Provision Stores

London	Telephone
(1) Cheong-Leen Supermarket (Mail Order) Tower House, 4–10 Tower Street, W.C.2	01–836-5378
(2) Chinese Emporium, 22 Rupert Street, W.1	01-437-0376
(3) Hongkong Emporium, 53 Rupert Street, W.1	01-437-8272
(4) Far Eastern Food Centre, 34 Greek Street, W.1	01-437-8737
(5) Dragon and Phoenix Co., 35 Balfe Street, N.1	01-837-0146
(6) Bombay Emporium, 12 Martello Road, E.8	01-254-8581
(7) Bombay Emporium, 70 Grafton Way, W.1	01-387-4514
(8) Loon Fung Chinese Emporium, 37 Gerrard Street, W.1	01-437-1922

Leeds

Shing Chong,
116 North Street, Leeds

Liverpool

(1) Wing Lee,
14 Nelson Street,
Liverpool, 1   Royal 7519

(2) Wei Sang Tong,
34 Nelson Street,
Liverpool, 1   Royal 4921

(3) Kwong Tai Yuen,
26 Nelson Street,
Liverpool, 1   Royal 2081

(4) Hing Lee Store,
31a Great George Street,
Liverpool 1

Birmingham
(1) Ling Yip Supermarket,
135–136 Digbeth,
Birmingham 5   021-643-6109

U.S.A.
(1) Oriental Food Shop,
1302 Amsterdam Avenue,
New York 27, N.Y.

(2) Mee Wah Lung Co.,
608 High Street, N.W.,
Washington, D.C.

(3) Red and Blue Co.,
2247 Wentworth Avenue,
Chicago 16, Illinois

(4) Superior Trading Co.,
867 Washington Street,
San Francisco 8, California

(5) Ti Hang Lung and Co.,
846 Grant Avenue,
San Francisco 8, California

(6) Berkeley Campus Co-op,
University of California,
Berkeley, California

(7) Yee Sing Chong Co.,
960–62 North Hill Street,
Los Angeles 12, California

(8) Sam Ward Co., Inc.,
957–61 North Hill Street,
Los Angeles 12, California

Index

More about Penguins

Penguinews, which appears every month, contains details of all the new books issued by Penguins as they are published. From time to time it is supplemented by *Penguins in Print*, which is a complete list of all available books published by Penguins. (There are well over three thousand of these.)

A specimen copy of *Penguinews* will be sent to you free on request, and you can become a subscriber for the price of the postage. For a year's issues (including the complete lists) please send 30p if you live in the United Kingdom, or 60p if you live elsewhere. Just write to Dept EP, Penguin Books Ltd, Harmondsworth, Middlesex, enclosing a cheque or postal order, and your name will be added to the mailing list.

Note: *Penguinews* and *Penguins in Print* are not available in the U.S.A. or Canada

South East Asian Food

Rosemary Brissenden

Indian and Chinese styles of cooking have since the war become gastronomically commonplace in Britain. This unusual book introduces the British or American cook to a much rarer tradition of cookery – the subtle styles of South East Asia.

Mrs Brissenden takes great care to make her subject clear. As well as recipes she gives detailed information about local herbs and spices, about utensils, and about conventions of work which won't be immediately obvious to the outsider. So you needn't be baffled by the mysterious customs of Indonesia, Malaysia or Thailand. Especially as the surprising message of South East Asia seems to be – relax!